FRESH INDIAN

SUNIL VIJAYAKAR

METRO BOOKS
NEW YORK

In memory of Leon

This 2008 edition published by Metro Books, by
arrangement with Hamlyn, a division of
Octopus Publishing Group Ltd.

Metro Books
122 Fifth Avenue
New York
NY10011

ISBN-13: 978-1-4351-0068-8
ISBN-10: 1-4351-0068-9

A catalogue record for this book is available from the
British Library

Printed and bound in China

1 3 5 7 9 10 8 6 4 2

Note

Standard level spoon measurements are used in all recipes.

1 tablespoon = one 15 ml spoon

1 teaspoon = one 5 ml spoon

The Food and Drug Administration advises that eggs should not be
consumed raw. This book contains dishes made with raw or lightly cooked
eggs. It is prudent for vulnerable people such as pregnant and nursing
mothers, those with compromised immune systems, the elderly, babies, and
young children to avoid uncooked or lightly cooked dishes made with eggs.
Once prepared, these dishes should be kept refrigerated and used promptly.

This book includes dishes made with nuts and nut derivatives. It is advisable
for those with known allergic reactions to nuts and nut derivatives and those
who may be potentially vulnerable to these allergies, such as pregnant and
nursing mothers, those with compromised immune systems, the elderly,
babies and children to avoid dishes made with nuts and nut oils. It is also
prudent to check the labels of pre-packaged ingredients for the possible
inclusion of nut derivatives.

Ovens should be preheated to the specified temperature—if using a
convection oven, follow the manufacturer's instructions for adjusting the
time and the temperature.

Contents

Introduction

For many, the idea of Indian food is one of high-fat, high-calorie dishes cooked in saturated fat and swimming with oil. But the truth is, Indian food can be light and healthy, with fresh flavors, fabulous colors and delicious textures. This book offers a modern approach to traditional Indian cooking, creating classic flavors and dishes using nutritious, low-fat ingredients and making use of healthy cooking techniques to achieve perfect, guilt-free, and authentic results.

There's a wide choice of both hot and mild dishes, some with light, fresh flavors, others with the mouthwatering, comforting texture of a slow-simmered dhal. The recipes have been designed with the modern cook in mind—making use of healthy ingredients that are fresh, delicious, and bursting with flavor.

A well-stocked pantry of basic ingredients and spices is essential. Most of these can be bought in large supermarkets, but I would urge you to visit an Indian or Asian market and stock up with a range of ingredients. Don't let yourself be intimidated by ingredients that may be new to you. Just make sure that you have everything laid out and on hand before you start to cook, and the rest will be easy.

At the end of the day, the main ingredient to have on hand is the love, enjoyment and passion for food, cooking, and eating. Don't be afraid to experiment so that you can understand the cooking techniques you employ, the ingredients you use, and the flavors and textures you create. As long as you approach your time in the kitchen in a relaxed, calm, and confident manner, following your own instincts and trusting your own palette, you can be confident of forging ahead to a delicious, healthy, and flavorful way of life to share with family and friends.

SUNIL VIJAYAKAR

Fresh and Healthy

The recipes in this book have all been devised with healthy eating in mind, using the healthiest ingredients and cooking techniques possible. They concentrate on cutting down on fat and salt, and using fresh, wholesome ingredients to provide you with the fuel you need to stay healthy and fit. Many dishes, such as the chutneys and salads, use raw fruit and vegetables, while others lightly cook them, tossing them with spices until they are just tender and still retain all their valuable nutrients. Low-fat cuts of meat and poultry are used, and there are plenty of dishes using healthy oily fish, which contain the essential fatty acids that are so important for good health.

Fat is the real villain in traditional Indian cooking, with most recipes starting with the frying of spices in *ghee* (clarified butter). However, it's easy to cut down on the fat and transform traditional dishes into healthy meals using simple, clever alternatives both in terms of ingredients and techniques. Unhealthy saturated ghee can be replaced with healthy monounsaturated fats such as sunflower or olive oils, and by using a nonstick pan, you'll find you need to use less oil. You can use low-fat cuts of meat, and remove the skin from chicken where most of its fat lies. Many high-fat ingredients used in classic Indian dishes, such as coconut milk and dairy products, can be replaced with low-fat versions, which still give rich results.

The recipes also utilize the most healthy cooking techniques, such as steaming, braising, baking, grilling, and stir-frying, and abandon the less healthy alternatives. For example, samosas are traditionally deep-fried, but here they are simply brushed with a tiny amount of oil and baked until crisp and golden. The results are just as delicious as the deep-fried version, and better for you.

For those who are trying to cut down on the amount of salt they eat, Indian food is the perfect choice. The generous use of spices, aromatics, and other flavorings allows you to produce wonderfully tasty dishes using very little salt. A squeeze of lime juice, a little extra turmeric, or a dash of tamarind water is often all that is needed to enhance and bring together the flavors of a dish. And the great thing about using less salt in cooking is that once you start using less, you'll find you don't need to use as much. Once you get used to the taste of less salty food, you will start to enjoy the fresh, clean taste of the other ingredients and flavorings so much more.

EATING THE INDIAN WAY Eating in India is all about coming together and sharing food with family and friends. A traditional meal is usually just one course—a casual affair comprising a selection of dishes placed on the table at the same time, with everyone serving themselves. There will be a choice of dishes, probably one meat, poultry, or fish dish, a vegetarian dish or

time of day, with or without a meal, and the desserts are just as good following a Western meal as an Indian one.

However you choose to use the recipes in this book, adopt the Indian approach to food—and submerge yourself in the joy of cooking, sharing, and eating good food.

Indian Flavors

The essence of Indian cooking lies in the ingredients you use and, in particular, in the wonderful combinations of spices, aromatics, herbs, and other flavorings that are blended and cooked to produce that unmistakable taste. A well-stocked pantry is essential, and although most of the ingredients can be found in large supermarkets, there's nothing like browsing among the shelves of Asian supermarkets and farmers' markets to inspire your culinary zeal and nurture your taste for the exotic. The smell of warm spices floating in the air, and the piles of glorious, fresh produce will be enough to have you running home and pulling pans out of the cabinets.

dhal, a rice dish, a bread, a bowl of yogurt or curd, and a selection of pickles and chutneys. For a vegetarian meal, the meat or fish dish will be replaced with a dhal or legume dish to provide protein, and for a more formal occasion or for larger numbers of people, more dishes will be served.

When we go to an Indian restaurant in the West, we often enjoy appetizers followed by a selection of main dishes, then a dessert, and the recipes in this book will allow you to do just that if you want to. However, don't feel restricted by tradition, enjoy these dishes in any way you like. You can enjoy a single dish on its own rather than as part of an Indian feast. Many of the vegetable dishes make perfect accompaniments for Western-style grilled meats and fish, or when you want to nibble, you can enjoy one of the snacks, such as Vegetable Samosas (*see page 22*) or Smoked Eggplant Dip (*see page 28*). The drinks are great at any

Spices

The imaginative use of spices characterizes Indian cuisine, so be sure to have the basics in your pantry. Quality is essential, so buy spices from a supplier with a rapid turnover—spices lose their flavor with age, and stale spices can spoil the taste of a dish. Ground spices lose their flavor within just a few months; therefore, it is usually better to buy whole spices and grind them as you need them. Some spices need to be roasted in a dry pan to bring out their aroma before grinding, while others can be used as they are.

Finally, store your spices well. They should be kept in tightly sealed containers, in a cool, dark place—and don't keep them for too long. If you find that you have very old spices in your pantry, it is well worth throwing them out and buying fresh ones—you'll really taste the difference.

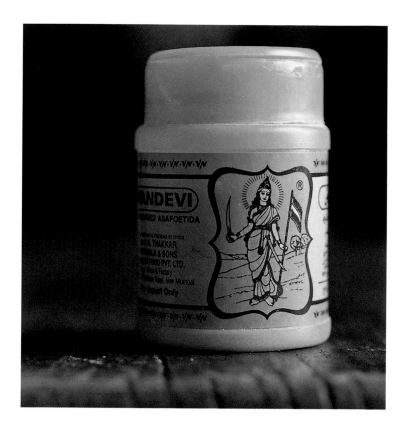

Whole seeds are often chewed as a breath freshener. There are three varieties: green, white, and black. The white pods are simply bleached green pods, and have a milder flavor. The black pods, which are used only in savory dishes, come from a related plant and have less aroma.

CASSIA Also known as Chinese cinnamon, cassia has a coarser appearance than cinnamon and a stronger flavor. If cassia is unavailable, cinnamon can be used instead. Pieces of the bark of the tree are available, or it may be ground.

CHILE Whole dried red chiles add a fiery heat, so use with caution. They are usually fried in hot oil to intensify their flavor. Dried chile flakes tend to have a milder flavor. Chili powders made from dried chiles vary in heat and are often labeled hot, medium, and mild. Cayenne pepper is fiery-hot, while paprika has a mild, slightly sweet, smoky flavor.

CINNAMON This sweet, warming spice is used to flavor sweet and savory dishes. It comes from the bark of a tree related to the laurel family and is available as sticks of rolled bark, or ground. If a cinnamon stick is used for flavoring, it should not be eaten once the dish is cooked.

CLOVES These very dark brown buds of an evergreen tree have a strong, pungent flavor and are used in small quantities, either whole or ground. If whole, do not eat once the dish is cooked.

CORIANDER The pale brown seed of the cilantro plant has a warm, burnt-orange aroma and may be used whole or ground. If grinding the seeds yourself, roast them first in a dry frying pan.

CUMIN Ubiquitous in Indian cooking, these small, elongated, pale brown seeds are available whole or ground. Cumin has a distinctive warm, pungent aroma and is usually fried first to intensify its flavor. Whole seeds may be roasted and sprinkled over a dish just before serving; if grinding the seeds yourself, roast them first in a dry frying pan.

AMCHOOR Also known as dried mango powder, this pale yellow powder made from dried green mangoes is used as a souring agent to bring out the flavor of other ingredients. It has a tart, fruity tang with a hint of sweetness and is widely available in Asian stores. If unavailable, you can use a squeeze of lemon or lime juice, or a dash of tamarind water instead.

ASAFOETIDA Available in lump or ground form from Asian stores, this is a plant resin with a very strong flavor and it is used in only very small quantities to give a subtle, garlicky aroma. Store in a very tightly sealed container.

CARDAMOM This sweetly aromatic spice, with a gingery, citrusy, almost eucalyptus-like fragrance, is widely used in both sweet and savory dishes. The pods may be added whole to rice, or split open and the seeds ground or used whole. The ground seeds are used in spice mixes, and are a key ingredient in garam masala.

CURRY LEAVES These small, dark green leaves have a distinctive "curry" aroma and are available fresh in Asian stores. (The fresh leaves freeze well.) Dried leaves are also available, although their flavor is not as good as that of the fresh leaves. Curry leaves are usually fried first, to release their flavor.

CURRY POWDERS AND PASTES Ready-made curry powders and pastes are an invention of the West but are, nonetheless, a useful ingredient in the Indian pantry. There are many different varieties, usually mild, medium and hot, as well as more specific mixes such as Madras curry powder, or tandoori spice mix. (*See separate entry for garam masala.*)

FENNEL SEEDS These small, pale greenish-brown seeds have a subtle, aniseed flavor. They are used as a flavoring in some dishes, and are often served after the end of the meal as a digestive aid and breath freshener.

FENUGREEK These tiny, smooth, yellowish seeds are used in pickles, chutneys, and vegetarian dishes.

GARAM MASALA Every household has its own variation of this classic spice mix, which is usually added toward the end of cooking time. A classic mix contains cardamom, cloves, cumin, peppercorns, cinnamon, and nutmeg. You can make your own at home, but very good ready-made mixes are available from supermarkets and Asian stores.

MACE This is the lacy covering of the nutmeg and is typically available ground. It has a similar flavor to nutmeg.

MUSTARD SEEDS An essential flavoring in Indian cooking—particularly dhals, vegetarian and rice dishes, and pickles—black, brown, and yellow mustard seeds are usually fried until they "pop" to achieve a mellow, nutty flavor. The crushed, whole seeds are extremely peppery and are sometimes added to pickles.

NIGELLA Also known as black onion seeds, or *kalonji*, these tiny, pungent seeds are most frequently used to flavor breads and pickles. They have quite a strong taste, so use them with caution.

NUTMEG Sweet and warmly aromatic, the whole spice comes as a round "nut" that is easy to grate on the fine blade of a grater. Although ground nutmeg is widely available, it quickly loses its taste and aroma, so it is better to buy the whole spice.

PEPPERCORNS Native to the Malabar coast, these tiny, pungent berries are a very popular flavoring. They may be used whole, crushed, or freshly ground. Avoid the ready-ground spice, because it loses the fresh, pungent bite of the whole spice.

SAFFRON Harvested from a special crocus, these deep-orange strands are used to impart a wonderfully musky fragrance to rice dishes and desserts. It is one of the most expensive spices, but only a little is needed, and it is well worth the cost. Avoid the powdered spice; the flavor is not as good and it may well have been adulterated.

TAMARIND Used as a souring agent to bring out and enhance the flavor of other ingredients, tamarind has a sharp, fruity tang. It is obtained from a pod and is usually available as a pulp, paste, or purée. The pulp needs to be soaked in hot water for several hours, then strained; the paste or purée can simply be dissolved in hot water.

TURMERIC This bright orange-yellow rhizome has a warm, musky flavor and is used in small quantities in vegetable and lentil dishes. The fresh spice can sometimes be found in Asian stores, but it is usually easier to buy the ground spice. The whole dried spice can also be found in Asian stores, but it is extremely hard and difficult to grind.

URAD DHAL Although this is a type of bean, in south Indian cooking urad dhal is used as a spice—fried first to release and intensify its nutty flavor.

Wet Spices and Aromatics

As well as the dried spices that can be found in the Indian pantry, there is also a selection of "wet" spices and aromatics that can be found in the fresh vegetable section of supermarket and Asian stores. Always look for unblemished, crisp and fresh ingredients.

CHILES Fresh jalapeño and red chiles are used to give heat and flavour to many Indian dishes—although it should be noted that not all Indian dishes contain chiles, and many spiced dishes can be mild. If you are not used to hot food, you can reduce the quantity of chile used to give a milder result. Jalapeños are more commonly used, although the riper red chiles are featured in many dishes. Much of the heat resides in the seeds and pith, so unless you want a fiery-hot dish, slit open the chiles and remove the seeds and pith before slicing or chopping the flesh. Always wash your hands with soap and water immediately after chopping chiles, and avoid touching the eyes, nose, mouth, and sensitive skin with chile-hands—the result will be exceedingly painful and uncomfortable.

GARLIC An absolute essential in Indian cooking, garlic is used with ginger and onion as the base of many classic dishes. There is no substitute for the flavor of fresh garlic, which is usually sliced, crushed, or grated and fried before other spices are added. Garlic can be grated into a paste and stored in an airtight jar in the refrigerator for up to 5 days.

GINGER Fresh root ginger is another indispensable aromatic and is used in both savory and sweet dishes. It has a fresh, zesty, peppery flavor; dried ground ginger is no substitute. Look for ginger with a smooth, light brown skin and peel it before dicing, grating, or slicing and cutting it into thin slivers. Store fresh ginger in the refrigerator for up to 2 weeks.

ONIONS Although the onion is usually considered a vegetable, it is such an essential flavoring ingredient in authentic Indian cooking (frequently used together with garlic and fresh ginger), that it deserves to be placed among the wet spices and aromatics. Many different types are used to different effects, including sweet yellow onions, mild red onions, and green onions. Store onions in a wire basket or a bowl in the kitchen at room temperature.

SHALLOTS These small, pungent members of the onion family are used in the same way as onions, particularly in southern and southwestern Indian cooking. To peel easily, simply slice each shallot in half lengthwise and remove the outer skin.

Herbs

Although fresh herbs do not play as large a role as spices in Indian cooking, they are still an integral part of the cuisine and impart a clean, fresh flavor to many dishes. They are usually added toward the end of cooking time or sprinkled over the finished dish.

BAY LEAVES The whole leaves are used occasionally in curries, and the dried, ground leaves are sometimes added to garam masala. In India, they are known as *tej patta* and are usually sold in their dried form.

CILANTRO Also known as *coriander*, fresh cilantro is an important ingredient in many savory dishes, salads, and chutneys. Its delicate leaves have a distinctive, fragrant aroma, and are usually added to dishes just before serving.

DILL Known as *suva* in India, distinctive, aniseed-scented dill is traditionally used in lentil dishes, but it also makes a good addition to rice. Store in the fridge wrapped in dampened paper towels for up to a week.

MINT Fresh, zesty mint is a popular ingredient in many dishes and chutneys. Although dried mint is widely available, it does not have the same tang as the fresh herb.

Pantry ingredients To make cooking completely stress-free, it is important to have a well-stocked pantry. Visit Asian supermarkets and farmers' markets for specialty Indian ingredients so that you can always substitute one ingredient for another. Restock regularly.

COCONUT Another essential ingredient, coconut milk and cream are added to savory dishes to add a rich sweetness and smooth, creamy texture. Although you can make your own coconut milk from the flesh of fresh coconuts, it is much easier to use the canned variety, of which there are healthier low-fat versions. Dried coconut is also commonly used and is available in packets. This is available plain or sweetened.

GRAM FLOUR Also known as *besan*, this golden flour (which is made from ground chickpeas) has a lovely, slightly nutty flavor and is used widely for thickening and binding as well as for making batters.

GROUND RICE, which is different from rice flour, is used in some Indian desserts. Because it is usually used in small amounts, you can make your own by grinding it in a coffee grinder.

LENTILS, PEAS, AND BEANS A plate of wholesome dhal is the staple of most Indians, and a good stock of dried and canned legumes is essential for the Indian kitchen. Dried lentils, split peas, and pale green mung beans need no soaking and do not take long to cook, while beans such as black-eyed peas, kidney beans, and chickpeas require lengthy soaking and long boiling until tender. For these "high maintenance" legumes, it is worth buying the canned variety. Look for beans canned in water, rather than brine, and always rinse them well before adding them to the pan.

NUTS AND SEEDS These play an important role in the Indian kitchen. Ground almonds and cashew nuts are a popular addition to savory dishes, while pale green pistachio nuts are often used in desserts. Poppy seeds are usually toasted to intensify their taste,

and are used to flavor curries. White poppy seeds are mainly used to thicken curries. If using from the pantry, you can always dry-roast them to bring out their flavor.

OILS Although *ghee* (clarified butter) is the traditional fat used for Indian cooking, the recipes in this book use healthier sunflower and olive oils. These oils have a mild flavor, so they do not interfere with the subtle flavorings of the dishes.

RICE By far the best choice of rice for serving with Indian food is basmati rice. Although it is a little more expensive than other long-grain rices, it has a wonderfully fragrant aroma and light fluffy texture when cooked. It benefits from rinsing or soaking in cold water before cooking.

RICE FLOUR is used in both sweet and savory dishes, including the classic southern pancakes, *dosas*, and the delicate steamed cakes, *idlis*.

ROSE WATER This delicate, fragrant flower essence is used to flavour Indian desserts and sweets. It can be found in most supermarkets, or in Asian and Middle Eastern stores. Rose petals are sometimes used to garnish Indian food.

SEMOLINA Coarse-ground semolina, known as *sooji* or *rava*, is available from Asian stores. It can be dry-roasted and is used to make the classic southwestern dish *uppama*, which is rather like a spiced vegetable pilaf and is a traditional breakfast dish. Do not buy the fine semolina used for puddings or sweets or you will end up with a sticky mess.

SWEETENERS Indian desserts and drinks are often very sweet, but many savory dishes also have a little sweetness to balance the other sharper flavors. Jaggery, a form of raw, lump, cane sugar sold in blocks or molds, is the classic Indian sugar, but other sweeteners, including palm sugar and honey, are used in the recipes in this book. Jaggery and palm sugar are both available from Asian stores. Soft brown sugar can be used if jaggery and palm sugar are not available.

Fresh Ingredients
The recipes in this book make use of the wonderful array of fresh ingredients available—from vibrant fruits and vegetables to fish, poultry, meat, and dairy products. The ingredients used here should be easy to find—if they are not available in a regular supermarket, visit your nearest Asian grocer.

COCONUT The grated flesh of fresh coconut is called for in many recipes, and some advice is needed on preparation. The easiest way to open the tough, brown-husked nut is either with a hammer, or by placing the coconut in a plastic bag and bashing it hard on a concrete floor. The flesh can then be pried from the

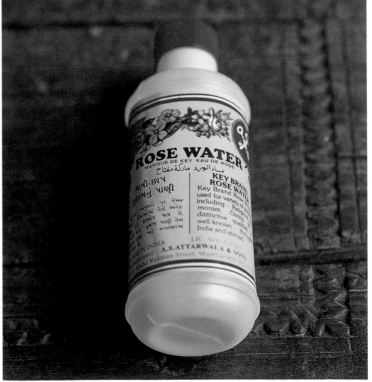

shell, the thin brown skin removed using a vegetable peeler, and the remaining flesh grated. If you cannot find fresh coconut, soak dried coconut in hot water for 5–10 minutes and then drain it.

DAIRY PRODUCTS These are not used as widely as they are in the Western kitchen, but there are a few indispensable ingredients. Yogurt is used to add creaminess to curries, as the base for marinades and dips, and also as an accompaniment. Its cooling flavor is the perfect foil for hot, chile-spiced dishes. Paneer, the fresh Indian cheese, is made from the curds of milk heated with lemon juice. Milk is a popular ingredient in drinks and desserts. Low-fat milk and yogurt are used in all the recipes in this book.

FRUITS These are widely used in sweet dishes, although some also play a role in savory dishes. The juice of lemons and limes is often used to bring out the flavor of other ingredients. Green mangoes, with their crisp, savory flesh are used as a vegetable, rather than a fruit, and dried fruits, such as dates and apricots, are used in both desserts and chutneys and relishes.

VEGETABLES Many of the vegetables used in the recipes in this book are classic Indian ingredients, such as eggplants, okra, cauliflower, spinach, peas, and tomatoes, while others, such as Japanese shiitake mushrooms, offer a more modern twist to classic recipes.

Equipment
When it comes to making the recipes in this book, there is very little that you will need in the way of essential equipment.

THE USUAL CUTTING BOARD AND SHARP KNIVES are needed for preparing ingredients. Be sure to use a plastic board for preparing fish, poultry, and meat because they are more hygienic and easier to clean.

A MORTAR AND PESTLE are essential for grinding spices. Electric spice grinders have, however, become inexpensive and will make much quicker work of the job.

A NONSTICK FRYING PAN will prove invaluable for low-fat frying, and also for dry-roasting spices. It can also be used in place of the traditional *tava*, the slightly concave, cast-iron griddle used for cooking flatbreads.

A HEAVY-BOTTOMED SAUCEPAN with a well-fitting lid is essential for making perfectly cooked, fluffy basmati rice.

A CHINESE WOK with a lid will also prove very useful. Its versatile shape—not unlike the traditional Indian *karahi*—means that it can double as a pan for healthy stir-frying, steaming, or braising.

Starters and snacks

Aloo chat

A classic snack in northern India, this piquant potato dish is traditionally eaten cold and has a fresh, tangy flavor. Pomegranate seeds make a stunning garnish and they add a lovely, clean, sweet-sharp flavor to the dish.

INGREDIENTS *1½ pounds potatoes, peeled and cut into ½-inch cubes* ‖ *3 tablespoons chopped cilantro leaves* ‖ *2 tablespoons chopped mint leaves* ‖ *1 jalapeño, deseeded and finely chopped* ‖ *½ teaspoon chili powder* ‖ *juice of 1 lemon* ‖ *½ cup water* ‖ *1 red onion, very finely chopped* ‖ *salt* ‖ *pomegranate seeds, to garnish*

ONE Boil the potatoes in a large saucepan of lightly salted water for 8–10 minutes or until just tender. Drain, cool thoroughly, and place in a large, shallow serving dish. **TWO** Place the cilantro and mint leaves, jalapeño, chili powder, and lemon juice in a small food processor with the measured water and blend until fairly smooth. Pour this mixture over the potatoes and stir in the onions. Season and toss to mix well. Serve cold or at room temperature, garnished with pomegranate seeds.

Serves 4

NUTRIENT ANALYSIS PER SERVING 150 cal – 636 kJ – 5 g protein – 34 g carbohydrates – 3 g sugars – 1 g fat – 0 g saturated fat – 3 g fiber – 21 mg sodium

HEALTHY TIP A small bowl of these tasty spiced potatoes makes a much healthier snack than a bag of chips or a couple of crackers. They taste delicious, are low in fat, and offer an excellent source of slow-release energy.

Vegetable samosas

Vegetable samosas These crispy pastries are classic Indian snack food – often cooked and sold on street corners, in bustling stations, or carried onto trains on large trays and sold to hungry travelers. In the West, they are popularly served as an appetizer and are delicious with a light, fragrant chutney.

INGREDIENTS *1 tablespoon sunflower oil ‖ 1 tablespoon medium curry powder ‖ 1 teaspoon amchoor (dried mango powder) ‖ ¾ pound boiled and roughly mashed potatoes ‖ 1 cup fresh peas ‖ 3 tablespoons finely chopped cilantro leaves ‖ salt ‖ 3 large sheets fresh filo dough, each approx. 12 inches x 8 inches ‖ light olive oil, to brush*

ONE Heat the sunflower oil in a large, nonstick frying pan and when hot add the curry and mango powder. Stir-fry for 10–15 seconds and then add the potatoes and peas. Stir and cook for 3–4 minutes, remove from the heat, stir in the chopped cilantro, season and set aside to cool. **TWO** Line a large baking sheet with nonstick parchment paper. **THREE** Working swiftly, place the 3 sheets of filo dough on top of each other and lay out flat on a work surface. Cut the filo dough sheets in half widthwise and then cut each half into 3 even strips to give you a total of 6 strips of filo per sheet. Lay the filo strips on a clean work surface and lightly brush each one with the olive oil. Place a teaspoon of the samosa filling at the bottom of each strip and then fold the pastry diagonally to enclose the filling and form a triangle. Press down on the pastry and fold again until you reach the end of the strip, leaving you with an enclosed filling in a triangular pastry parcel. Repeat with the remaining strips and filling to make 18 samosas. Place the samosas on the prepared baking sheet and bake for 15–20 minutes in a preheated oven, 375°F, or until crisp and golden. Remove from the oven and serve immediately with a tomato sauce or Cilantro, Mint, and Coconut Chutney (*SEE PAGE 129*).

Makes 18

NUTRIENT ANALYSIS PER SAMOSA 47 cal – 199 kJ – 1 g protein – 8 g carbohydrates – 1 g sugars – 1 g fat – 0.2 g saturated fat – 1 g fiber – 29 mg sodium

HEALTHY TIP Traditionally, samosas are deep-fried, but here they are simply brushed with a little oil and baked in the oven until crisp and golden. This method gives delicious results and is much healthier than the deep-fried version.

Minted lamb kebabs

These little spiced meatballs flavored with fresh herbs make a perfect snack to serve with drinks before dinner. Because they can be prepared ahead and popped into the oven at the last minute, they're great for quick and easy entertaining. Serve with Tamarind and Red Pepper Chutney (*SEE PAGE 125*) for dipping.

INGREDIENTS *1 tablespoon chickpea flour (besan or gram flour)* ‖ *1¼ pounds finely ground lamb* ‖ *5 tablespoons finely chopped mint leaves* ‖ *3 tablespoons finely chopped cilantro leaves* ‖ *2 jalapeños, seeded and finely chopped* ‖ *2 teaspoons ground cumin* ‖ *1 teaspoon ground coriander* ‖ *salt and freshly ground black pepper* ‖ *½ small egg, lightly beaten* ‖ *sunflower oil, to brush*

ONE Place the chickpea flour, ground lamb, chopped mint and cilantro leaves, jalapeño and the ground spices in a mixing bowl. Season, add the egg and, using your hands, mix until very well combined. Cover and chill for 2–3 hours, or overnight if time permits. **TWO** Line a large baking sheet with parchment paper. Divide the lamb mixture into 12 pieces and shape each one into a round ball. Flatten slightly and place on the prepared baking sheet. Brush lightly with the oil and bake in a preheated oven, 375° F, for 12–15 minutes or until cooked through. Remove and serve immediately as an appetizer with drinks.

Serves 4

NUTRIENT ANALYSIS PER SERVING 307 cal – 1285 kJ – 36 g protein – 3 g carbohydrates – 0 g sugars – 17 g fat – 7 g saturated fat – 1 g fiber – 158 mg sodium

HEALTHY TIP Lamb is a quite fatty meat, so either go for ground lamb with a low fat content, or choose a low-fat cut of lamb and grind it yourself (or ask your butcher to grind it for you).

Chilled yogurt, cucumber, and mint soup

Cool and refreshing yogurt soup, spiced with cumin and chile, makes a gentle start to a spicy Indian meal. It has a slightly sharp, piquant flavor, and the addition of finely chopped fresh cucumber and tomato gives it a lovely bite.

INGREDIENTS *2½ cups low-fat plain yogurt, plus a little extra, to drizzle* ‖ *2½ cups fresh vegetable stock* ‖ *½ teaspoon finely grated fresh ginger root* ‖ *½ teaspoon ground cumin* ‖ *¼ teaspoon chili powder* ‖ *1 small cucumber* ‖ *2 plum tomatoes* ‖ *¼ cup finely chopped mint leaves* ‖ *salt and freshly ground black pepper* ‖ *roasted cumin seeds, to sprinkle*

ONE Place the yogurt, stock, ginger, cumin, and chili powder in a food processor and blend until smooth. Transfer to a mixing bowl. **TWO** Finely dice the cucumber; seed and finely dice the tomatoes and add to the yogurt mixture with the chopped mint. Season well and stir to combine evenly. Cover and chill in the refrigerator for 30 minutes before serving. Drizzle with a little yogurt and sprinkle some roasted cumin seeds over the top before serving.

Serves 4

NUTRIENT ANALYSIS PER SERVING 113 cal – 478 kJ – 10 g protein – 15 g carbohydrates – 15 g sugars – 2 g fat – 1 g saturated fat – 1 g fiber – 363 mg sodium

HEALTHY TIP Low-fat yogurt has a wonderful taste and texture, so it makes the natural choice for a dish such as this. Be on the lookout for live yogurt, which contains healthy bacteria that can help improve digestive health.

Green chicken kebabs

Fragrant and bursting with flavor, these succulent chicken skewers are low in fat and make an excellent light lunch or dinner dish when served with a crisp cucumber and red onion salad.

INGREDIENTS *½ cup low-fat plain yogurt* ‖ *2 garlic cloves, crushed* ‖ *2 teaspoons finely grated fresh ginger root* ‖ *2 teaspoons ground cumin* ‖ *1 teaspoon ground coriander* ‖ *1 jalapeño, finely chopped* ‖ *large handful of freshly chopped cilantro leaves* ‖ *small handful of chopped mint leaves* ‖ *juice of 2 limes* ‖ *sea salt* ‖ *4 chicken breasts, skinned and boned*

TO SERVE *lime halves*

ONE Place the yogurt, garlic, ginger, cumin, coriander, jalapeño, chopped herbs, and lime juice in a blender and blend until fairly smooth. Season lightly. **TWO** Cut the chicken into bite-sized pieces and place in a large mixing bowl. Pour the spice mixture over and toss to coat evenly. Cover with plastic wrap and marinate in the refrigerator for 4–6 hours, or overnight if time permits. **THREE** When ready to cook, preheat the grill to medium-high and thread the chicken pieces onto 8 presoaked bamboo skewers. Cook over a preheated grill for 8–10 minutes, turning frequently, until cooked through and lightly browned. Remove and serve immediately with lime halves to squeeze on top and a cucumber and red onion salad on the side.

Serves 4

NUTRIENT ANALYSIS PER SERVING 175 cal – 737 kJ – 30 g protein – 3 g carbohydrates – 2 g sugars – 5 g fat – 1 g saturated fat – 0 g fiber – 118 mg sodium

HEALTHY TIP Most of the fat in chicken is found in or just under the skin, so using skinless chicken breasts is the obvious healthy option. Marinating the meat before cooking ensures that the cooked kebabs are moist and juicy despite being low in fat.

Smoked eggplant dip

Charring eggplant over an open flame before baking it gives the meltingly tender flesh a smoky flavor. The addition of hot peppers, aromatic garlic, and fragrant cilantro is all that is needed to make a delicious dip to serve with drinks before dinner.

INGREDIENTS *1 large, firm eggplant* ‖ *1 shallot, finely chopped* ‖ *1 garlic clove, crushed* ‖ *1 jalapeño, finely chopped* ‖ *¼ cup chopped cilantro leaves* ‖ *1 plum tomato, finely diced* ‖ *½ cup low-fat plain yogurt* ‖ *salt* ‖ *crisp pappadams or grilled flatbreads, to serve*

ONE Hold the eggplants over an open flame using long tongs (on the range or over a barbecue) and turn and cook until the skin is blistered and charred. Transfer to a baking sheet and cook in a preheated oven, 400°F, for 20–25 minutes or until softened. **TWO** Remove the eggplant from the oven and carefully peel off the skin over a large bowl, saving any juices. Roughly chop up the remaining flesh and place in a food processor with the saved juices. Blend until fairly smooth and then transfer to a bowl. Stir in the shallot, garlic, jalapeño, cilantro, tomato, and yogurt. Season well and chill for 3–4 hours to allow the flavors to develop. Serve the dip with crisp pappadams or grilled flatbreads.

Serves 4

NUTRIENT ANALYSIS PER SERVING 42 cal – 176 kJ – 3 g protein – 6 g carbohydrates – 6 g sugars – 1 g fat – 0 g saturated fat – 2 g fiber – 36 mg sodium

HEALTHY TIP Dips can often be high in fat, but using low-fat yogurt as the base makes this a healthy snack. If you're looking to reduce the amount of fat you eat, serve the dip with grilled flatbread, rather than deep-fried crispy pappadams.

Beet and cilantro salad

Beautifully flavored and richly colored, this refreshing salad, packed with texture and taste, makes a terrific accompaniment to any meal.

INGREDIENTS *4 large beets, cooked* ‖ *2 teaspoons cumin seeds* ‖ *1 teaspoon black onion seeds (nigella)* ‖ *1 teaspoon coriander seeds* ‖ *¼ teaspoon mild chili powder* ‖ *2 tablespoons low-fat coconut milk* ‖ *1 cup low-fat plain yogurt* ‖ *handful of cilantro leaves* ‖ *2 tablespoons roasted pumpkin seeds* ‖ *sea salt*

ONE Peel the beets and cut them into bite-sized pieces. Place in a large serving bowl. **TWO** Put a frying pan over medium heat and place the cumin, nigella, and coriander seeds in it. Dry-roast the spices for 2–3 minutes until they release their aromas. Place in a mortar and pestle and lightly crush them. Transfer to a small mixing bowl with the chili powder, coconut milk, and yogurt. Stir to mix well. **THREE** Roughly chop the cilantro leaves and add to the beets with the pumpkin seeds. Drizzle with the yogurt mixture, season, and serve immediately.

Serves 4

NUTRIENT ANALYSIS PER SERVING 93 cal – 394 kJ – 5 g protein – 13 g carbohydrates – 11 g sugars – 3 g fat – 1 g saturated fat – 3 g fiber – 120 mg sodium

HEALTHY TIP Beets are high in antioxidants, making it excellent for boosting the immune system, fighting infection, and detoxifying your body, and they are also a good source of iron. In traditional herbalism, beets are often recommended as a blood builder.

Grilled corn with chili and lime
Char-grilling corn gives it a smoky flavor, which is set off by the spicy chili and sharp, tangy lime juice. Served piping hot, it makes a perfect snack to serve with drinks.

INGREDIENTS *4 ears of corn* ‖ *1 tablespoon coarse chili powder* ‖ *1 tablespoon sea salt* ‖ *2 limes, halved*

ONE Remove the husks and silk from the corn; reserve the husks. **TWO** Mix together the coarse chili powder and sea salt and place on a small plate or saucer. Cut the limes in half and set aside. **THREE** Cook the corn over a medium heat over a grill or under a medium-hot broiler for 4–5 minutes, turning them so that they cook all over, until the corn is lightly charred in places. Remove from the heat, dip a lime half in the chili mixture and squeeze and spread it over the corn to coat evenly. Repeat with the remaining corn, lime and chili mixture. Place the corn on the reserved husks and eat immediately.

Serves 4

NUTRIENT ANALYSIS PER SERVING 49 cal – 206 kJ – 2 g protein – 9 g carbohydrates – 1 g sugars – 1 g fat – 0.1 g saturated fat – 2 g fiber – 1964 mg sodium

HEALTHY TIP This virtually fat-free snack makes a great alternative to spiced nuts or other high-fat snacks. The corn is quite salty though, so be careful if you are on a low-sodium diet.

Tomato, mixed sprouts, and cucumber salad

Mixed sprouts are widely available from any good farmers' market or health food store. They come in various mixtures, from sprouted mung beans, to red lentil and chickpea sprouts, and have a crisp, refreshing texture when they are used raw in salads.

INGREDIENTS *1 pint cherry or grape tomatoes, roughly chopped* ‖ *1¼ pounds mixed fresh sprouted beans and lentils* ‖ *1 small red onion, very finely diced* ‖ *4 small Lebanese cucumbers, thinly sliced or finely chopped* ‖ *1 tablespoon light olive oil* ‖ *juice of 1 lemon* ‖ *1 teaspoon roasted cumin seeds* ‖ *3 tablespoons chopped mint leaves* ‖ *2 tablespoons chopped cilantro leaves* ‖ *salt and freshly ground black pepper*

ONE Place the tomatoes in a mixing bowl. Rinse and drain the mixed sprouts and add them to the tomatoes with the red onion and cucumber. **TWO** Mix together the olive oil, lemon juice, and cumin seeds and pour over the salad. Stir in the chopped herbs and season well before serving.

Serves 4

NUTRIENT ANALYSIS PER SERVING 97 cal – 405 kJ – 6 g protein – 10 g carbohydrates – 7 g sugars – 4 g fat – 1 g saturated fat – 10 g fiber – 16 mg sodium

HEALTHY TIP Sprouted beans and lentils are packed with health-giving minerals and vitamins, and sprouting actually appears to boost the nutritional content of some beans and lentils.

Paneer kachumber

This traditional, refreshing salad combines fresh and zesty flavors with the mild Indian cheese, paneer. Paneer is widely available in large supermarkets and Asian stores, although it can easily be made at home, simply by heating milk with a little lemon juice, then separating out and pressing the curds.

INGREDIENTS *2 x 8 ounces packages paneer (Indian cheese made from milk)* ‖ *sunflower oil, for brushing*

KACHUMBER *2 plum tomatoes, seeded and very finely chopped* ‖ *1 roasted red pepper from a jar (3½ ounces), drained and very finely chopped* ‖ *1 shallot, peeled and very finely diced* ‖ *½ cup sprouted mung beans* ‖ *¼ cup very finely diced cucumber* ‖ *3 tablespoons finely chopped cilantro leaves* ‖ *1 teaspoon finely grated lime zest* ‖ *juice of 2 limes* ‖ *1 tablespoon sunflower oil or light olive oil* ‖ *1 teaspoon honey* ‖ *salt and chili powder, to season* ‖ *cilantro leaves, to garnish*

ONE Cut the paneer into bite-sized cubes. Brush lightly with oil. Heat a nonstick, ridged griddle pan over high heat and cook the paneer cubes in batches for 1–2 minutes on all sides. Remove from the heat and transfer to 4 warmed serving plates and keep warm. **TWO** Place the tomatoes, red pepper, shallot, mung beans, cucumber, and cilantro in a small bowl. Mix together the lime zest and juice, oil, and honey and pour over the vegetable mixture. Season and toss to mix well. Spoon this mixture over and around each serving of griddled paneer, garnish with fresh cilantro leaves, and serve warm or at room temperature.

Serves 4

NUTRIENT ANALYSIS PER SERVING 165 cal – 694 kJ – 17 g protein – 8 g carbohydrates – 8 g sugars – 8 g fat – 3 g saturated fat – 2 g fiber – 438 mg sodium

HEALTHY TIP Paneer is an excellent source of calcium, which is essential for healthy bones and teeth. It is also a good source of protein, so it makes a nutritious choice for vegetarians.

Meat and poultry

Grilled spicy chicken

Grilled chicken breasts make an ideal quick, midweek supper—just toss together the marinade and chicken before you go to work and leave in the refrigerator, ready for grilling when you get home.

INGREDIENTS *4 chicken breast fillets, skinned* ‖ *juice of 1 lemon* ‖ *sea salt*

MARINADE *1 teaspoon amchoor (dried mango powder)* ‖ *1 teaspoon crushed fenugreek seeds* ‖ *1 teaspoon garam masala* ‖ *2 teaspoons finely grated fresh ginger root* ‖ *2 teaspoons finely grated garlic* ‖ *1 tablespoon chili powder* ‖ *1 teaspoon ground cumin* ‖ *1 teaspoon ground coriander* ‖ *1 cup low-fat plain yogurt* ‖ *lime wedges, to serve*

ONE Slash each breast diagonally, 3–4 times and place them in a shallow, nonreactive dish. Pour the lemon juice over top and season with the salt. Cover and set aside. **TWO** Meanwhile, place all the marinade ingredients in a food processor and blend until smooth. Pour this mixture over the chicken, cover and allow to marinate in the refrigerator for 2–3 hours. **THREE** When you are ready to cook, remove the chicken breasts from the marinade and place them on a grill rack. Cook over a medium-hot grill for 15 minutes, turning them halfway through, or until they are cooked and lightly charred on the edges. Serve immediately with a crisp salad and serve garnished with lime wedges.

Serves 4

NUTRIENT ANALYSIS PER SERVING 216 cal – 911 kJ – 36 g protein – 6 g carbohydrate – 5 g sugars – 6 g fat – 2 g saturated fat – 0 g fiber – 175 mg sodium

HEALTHY TIP Grilling is a really healthy cooking method because it requires no extra fat, and the thick yogurt marinade ensures that the chicken stays moist during cooking.

South Indian pepper chicken
Spiced with peppercorns rather than chiles, this creamy curry will be popular with the whole family. Fresh ginger and garlic give it a warming, spicy aroma. Serve with a refreshing salad to complement the creamy sauce.

INGREDIENTS *1 tablespoon sunflower oil* ‖ *1 bay leaf* ‖ *4 cloves* ‖ *½ teaspoon crushed cardamom seeds* ‖ *2 teaspoons crushed black peppercorns* ‖ *1 teaspoon finely grated fresh ginger root* ‖ *2 teaspoons finely grated garlic* ‖ *1¼ pounds boneless, skinless chicken breasts, cut into bite-sized pieces* ‖ *½ cup water or chicken stock* ‖ *½ teaspoon turmeric* ‖ *1½ cups low-fat plain yogurt* ‖ *salt*

ONE Heat the oil in a large nonstick frying pan and when hot add the bay leaf, cloves, crushed cardamom seeds, and peppercorns. Stir-fry for 30 seconds, then add the ginger, garlic, and the chicken. Stir-fry over a medium heat for 4–5 minutes before adding the water or stock and the turmeric. Season. **TWO** Bring to a boil, cover, reduce the heat, and simmer gently for 10–12 minutes or until the chicken is tender and cooked through. Remove from heat, drizzle with the yogurt so that it is partially stirred in and serve.

Serves 4

NUTRIENT ANALYSIS PER SERVING 266 cal – 1119 kJ – 40 g protein – 7 g carbohydrates – 7 g sugars – 9 g fat – 2 g saturated fat – 0 g fiber – 190 mg sodium

HEALTHY TIP Adding low-fat yogurt gives this dish a rich creaminess, with none of the fat that comes with cream, ground almonds, or coconut – which are all popular ingredients in many Indian curries.

Green chicken curry

Sweet and spicy, this chicken curry cooked in a rich and creamy coconut sauce is a real treat. Jaggery and palm sugar are available from Asian stores, but if you can't find them, you can use soft brown sugar instead.

INGREDIENTS *1 tablespoon sunflower oil ‖ 1 onion, finely chopped ‖ 3 garlic cloves, finely chopped ‖ 2 teaspoons finely grated fresh ginger root ‖ large handful of cilantro leaves, chopped ‖ ¼ cup chopped mint leaves ‖ 1 jalapeño, chopped ‖ ¼ teaspoon crushed cardamom seeds ‖ 2 teaspoons ground cumin ‖ 2 teaspoons ground coriander ‖ 1 teaspoon jaggery or palm sugar, grated ‖ 1¾ cups low-fat coconut milk ‖ 1¼ pounds boneless, skinless chicken thighs, cut into small pieces ‖ scant 1 cup water ‖ salt and freshly ground black pepper ‖ Lebanese cucumber, cut into fine strips, to garnish*

ONE Heat the oil in a large saucepan or wok, add the onion, and cook over medium heat for 5–6 minutes, stirring often. **TWO** Meanwhile, place the garlic, ginger, cilantro leaves, mint leaves, jalapeño, cardamom, ground cumin, ground coriander, jaggery or palm sugar, and coconut milk in a food processor and blend until smooth. **THREE** Add the chicken to the onion and cook over high heat for 4–5 minutes, stirring often, until sealed and lightly browned. Pour in the coconut mixture and add the water. Season well and bring to a boil. Reduce the heat, cover, and cook gently for 20–25 minutes or until the chicken is tender and cooked through. Serve immediately with the Lebanese cucumber garnish and steamed basmati rice.

Serves 4

NUTRIENT ANALYSIS PER SERVING 344 cal – 1436 kJ – 31 g protein – 10 g carbohydrate – 8 g sugars – 20 g fat – 9 g saturated fat – 1 g fiber – 250 mg sodium

HEALTHY TIP Coconut milk is high in fat, so it should be used in moderation if you're watching the amount of fat you eat. However, this recipe uses low-fat coconut milk, making it a little bit healthier.

Pork kheema with peas

Warm fragrant cilantro, aromatic garlic, and spicy chiles are the perfect partners for mildly flavored pork. This tasty dish, in a rich tomato sauce, is quick and easy to make and is great for a simple midweek dinner, served with flatbreads or plain rice.

INGREDIENTS *1 tablespoon sunflower oil* ‖ *2 garlic cloves, finely chopped* ‖ *2 jalapeños, seeded and finely chopped* ‖ *1 teaspoon ground coriander* ‖ *l pound ground pork* ‖ *2½ cups fresh or frozen peas* ‖ *3 tablespoons medium curry paste* ‖ *3 tablespoons tomato purée* ‖ *2 tomatoes, finely chopped* ‖ *1 teaspoon raw sugar* ‖ *1 cup boiling water* ‖ *2 tablespoons low-fat plain yogurt* ‖ *large handful of chopped cilantro leaves* ‖ *salt*

ONE Heat the oil in a large, nonstick wok or frying pan; when it is hot, add the garlic, jalapeños, ground coriander and pork. Stir-fry over high heat for 4–5 minutes until the meat is sealed and lightly browned. **TWO** Stir in the peas, curry paste, tomato purée, chopped tomatoes and sugar. Stir and cook for 3–4 minutes and then add the water. Bring to a boil, cover, reduce the heat, and cook gently for 8–10 minutes or until the meat is tender. Remove from heat, stir in the yogurt and the chopped cilantro, season, and serve with flatbreads or plain rice.

Serves 4

NUTRIENT ANALYSIS PER SERVING 362 cal – 1513 kJ – 35 g protein – 18 g carbohydrate – 10 g sugars – 17 g fat – 4 g saturated fat – 8 g fiber – 449 mg sodium

HEALTHY TIP Frozen peas often contain more nutrients than fresh. They are frozen quickly after picking and shelling, so more of their nutrients are retained than in fresh peas, which are often sold days after picking, having been transported, stored in warehouses, and finally placed on supermarket or farmers' market shelves.

Marinated spiced lamb
Spice-coated racks of lamb, baked until tender and then cut into "cutlets," make an impressive main dish.

INGREDIENTS *4 French-trimmed racks of lamb (each rack with 3–4 ribs)* ‖ *3 garlic cloves, crushed* ‖ *2 teaspoons finely grated fresh ginger root* ‖ *2 tablespoons white wine vinegar* ‖ *6 tablespoons very finely chopped mint leaves* ‖ *2 teaspoons ground cumin* ‖ *2 teaspoons ground coriander* ‖ *1 teaspoon chili powder* ‖ *½ cup low-fat plain yogurt* ‖ *salt*

ONE Place the racks of lamb in a shallow, nonreactive dish in a single layer. Put the garlic, ginger, vinegar, mint, cumin, coriander, chili powder and yogurt in a food processor and blend until smooth. Season, then pour this mixture over the lamb to coat it evenly. Cover and chill in the refrigerator for 3–4 hours or overnight if time permits. **TWO** Lay the lamb on a nonstick baking sheet and place it in a preheated oven, 400°F, and cook for 20–25 minutes or longer if you prefer it well done. Remove from the oven, cover with foil, and allow the lamb to stand and rest for 5–10 minutes before cutting it into "cutlets" and serving with Spiced Lemon Rice (*SEE PAGE 96*).

Serves 4

NUTRIENT ANALYSIS PER SERVING 432 cal – 1797 kJ – 42 g protein – 4 g carbohydrates – 3 g sugars – 28 g fat – 14 g saturated fat – 0 g fiber – 133 mg sodium

HEALTHY TIP Marinating meat before cooking not only imparts a wonderful flavor, but also ensures moist, juicy results. Oil-based marinades can introduce extra fat, but this one using low-fat yogurt keeps down the fat content of the dish.

Beef brochettes with mango salsa

Chunky beef skewers, marinated overnight, then grilled and served with a fresh salsa make a delicious lunch or supper dish. To make a substantial meal of it, serve the brochettes with a crunchy salad or salsa and chapatis for wrapping around the spicy chunks of meat.

INGREDIENTS *1 pound beef fillet, cut into bite-sized cubes*

MARINADE *½ cup low-fat yogurt ‖ ½ small onion, roughly chopped ‖ 2 teaspoons finely grated fresh root ginger ‖ 2 teaspoons finely grated garlic ‖ 3 tablespoons tomato purée ‖ 1 tablespoon curry powder (medium) ‖ 2 tablespoons chopped cilantro leaves ‖ ½ teaspoon salt*

SALSA *1 ripe mango, finely diced ‖ ½ small red onion, finely diced ‖ 2 tablespoons each of chopped cilantro and mint leaves ‖ 1 red chile, deseeded and finely chopped ‖ juice of 2 limes ‖ salt*

ONE Place the beef in a nonreactive bowl. Blend all the marinade ingredients together in a food processor until smooth and pour over the meat. Cover and marinate overnight in the refrigerator. **TWO** Make the salsa by combining all the ingredients in a bowl and seasoning to taste. **THREE** Thread the marinated meat on to 8 metal skewers (or presoaked bamboo ones) and cook under a hot broiler for 12–15 minutes turning halfway through cooking until the meat is cooked to your liking. Remove and let rest for 3–4 minutes before serving with the mango salsa.

Serves 4

NUTRIENT ANALYSIS PER SERVING 225 cal – 949 kJ – 29 g protein – 13 g carbohydrates – 12 g sugars – 7 g fat – 3 g saturated fat – 1 g fiber – 167 mg sodium

HEALTHY TIP Beef is a great source of iron, which is essential for healthy red blood cells. The cut used here is tender and low in fat.

Beef kofta curry

Small, spicy balls of ground beef cooked in a smooth, spicy sauce make a warming dinner. Serve with with Indian flatbreads and a fresh Indian salad or salsa. Wrap the koftas and salad up in the bread for an informal meal.

INGREDIENTS *1¼ pounds lean ground beef ‖ 1 teaspoon finely grated fresh ginger root ‖ 2 teaspoons fennel seeds ‖ 1 teaspoon ground cinnamon ‖ 1 teaspoon turmeric ‖ 2 tablespoons mild curry powder ‖ 17 ounces crushed tomatoes ‖ salt and freshly ground black pepper*

TO GARNISH *low-fat yogurt to drizzle and mint leaves to scatter*

ONE Place the ground beef and ginger in a large mixing bowl. Roughly crush the fennel seeds in a mortar and pestle and add to the mixture with the cinnamon. Season and, using your hands, mix thoroughly. Form the mixture into small, walnut-sized balls and set aside. **TWO** Place the turmeric, curry powder, and tomatoes in a wide, nonstick saucepan and bring to a boil. Season, reduce the heat, and carefully place the meatballs in the sauce. Cover and cook gently for 15–20 minutes, stirring and turning the meatballs around occasionally, until they are cooked through. Remove from the heat, drizzle with the low-fat yogurt, and scatter with the mint leaves. Serve with chapatis or other flatbreads and salad.

Serves 4

NUTRIENT ANALYSIS PER SERVING 212 cal – 893 kJ – 32 g protein – 5 g carbohydrates – 4 g sugars – 7 g fat – 3 g saturated fat – 1 g fiber – 142 mg sodium

HEALTHY TIP Ground beef can be very high in fat, so always check the label carefully and go for the lowest fat option.

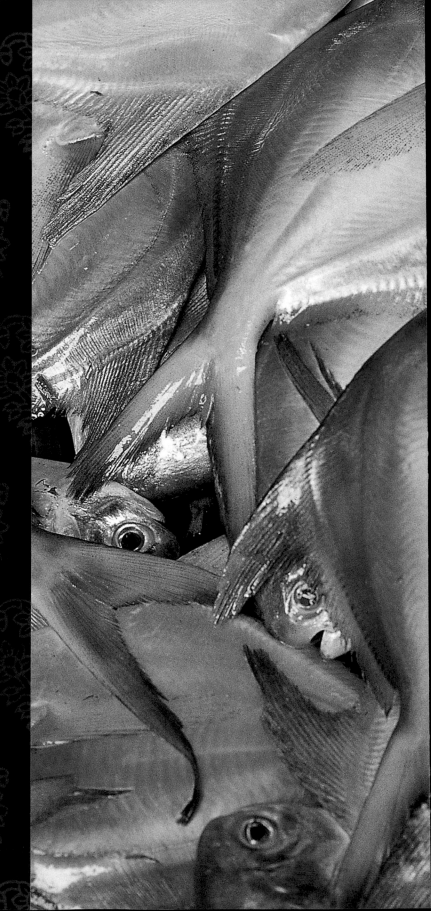

Fish and seafood

Crispy grilled red masala mackerel

In India, the word masala simply means spice mixture, and the actual blend can vary enormously, depending on the dish it is to be cooked in and where in the country it originates. Here, a wet paste is used and spread over the fish as a spicy marinade before grilling.

INGREDIENTS *4 fresh mackerel, each around 8–10 ounces, cleaned and gutted*

RED MASALA PASTE *1 tablespoon sunflower oil* ‖ *1 teaspoon finely grated fresh ginger root* ‖ *2 teaspoons finely grated garlic* ‖ *2 red chiles, deseeded and very finely chopped* ‖ *1 teaspoon chili powder* ‖ *½ teaspoon turmeric* ‖ *1 teaspoon ground cumin* ‖ *1 teaspoon ground coriander* ‖ *¼ cup tomato purée* ‖ *1 teaspoon grated jaggery or palm sugar* ‖ *juice of 2 lemons* ‖ *salt*

TO SERVE *red onion rings, sliced cucumber and sliced tomatoes*

ONE Place the fish on a cutting board and make 4–5 deep diagonal slices on each side. **TWO** Make the paste by placing all the ingredients in a food processor with a couple of tablespoons of water and mixing until fairly smooth. Season well and spread this mixture over the fish, making sure it gets into the slits on either side. **THREE** Place the fish on a grill rack and cook under a hot broiler for 6–8 minutes on each side until cooked through and lightly charred on the edges. Serve immediately with the red onion rings, sliced cucumber, and sliced tomatoes.

Serves 4

NUTRIENT ANALYSIS PER SERVING 403 cal – 1676 kJ – 31 g protein – 7 g carbohydrates – 5 g sugars – 28 g fat – 5 g saturated fat – 0 g fiber – 265 mg sodium

HEALTHY TIP The spices used in this recipe have a range of therapeutic properties, including boosting the immune system, improving circulation, improving mood, and reducing inflammation.

Bengali-style mustard fish

In Bengal in eastern India, there is a plentiful supply of fish from the Bay of Bengal, and many different ways of cooking it. Here, white fish is simply spiced with mustard, turmeric, and chile and baked until just cooked through.

INGREDIENTS *1 teaspoon turmeric* ‖ *1 teaspoon chili powder* ‖ *2 tablespoons whole grain mustard* ‖ *2 teaspoons black mustard seeds* ‖ *2 tablespoons sunflower oil* ‖ *juice of 1 lime* ‖ *salt* ‖ *4 thick halibut or cod fillets, each about 8 ounces, skinned* ‖ *chopped cilantro leaves, to garnish*

ONE Line a baking sheet with nonstick parchment paper. **TWO** Using a mortar and pestle, crush the turmeric, chili powder, whole grain mustard, and black mustard seeds until fairly well combined. Add the oil and lime juice and season well. Stir to mix thoroughly. **THREE** Place the fish fillets on the prepared baking sheet. Spread the mustard mixture over the fish and place in a preheated oven, 400°F, and cook for 15–20 minutes or until cooked through. Remove from the oven and serve immediately, garnished with chopped cilantro.

Serves 4

NUTRIENT ANALYSIS PER SERVING 228 cal – 958 kJ – 32 g protein – 1 g carbohydrates – 0 g sugars – 11 g fat – 1 g saturated fat – 0 g fiber – 274 mg sodium

HEALTHY TIP Mustard, like many spices, is reputed to have health-giving properties. It is said to stimulate the appetite and digestion, and is also believed to help clear the sinuses.

Mustard-grilled sardines
Perfect for a summer barbecue or a simple lunch or dinner, these deliciously spicy sardines are great served simply with a fresh salad and lemon wedges.

INGREDIENTS *12 medium-sized sardines* ‖ *1 tablespoon whole grain mustard* ‖ *juice of 2 lemons* ‖ *1 teaspoon chili powder* ‖ *1 teaspoon garam masala* ‖ *salt*

ONE Put the sardines on a large work surface and, using a sharp knife, make 2–3 diagonal slashes on both sides of each fish. **TWO** In a small bowl, mix together the mustard, lemon juice, chili powder, and garam masala. Season, then spread this mixture over the fish. **THREE** Place the sardines on a grill rack and cook under a medium-hot broiler for 3–4 minutes on each side or until cooked through. Serve hot with wedges of lemon.

Serves 4

NUTRIENT ANALYSIS PER SERVING 257 cal – 1078 kJ – 32 g protein – 1 g carbohydrates – 1 g sugars – 14 g fat – 4 g saturated fat – 0 g fiber – 249 mg sodium

HEALTHY TIP Sardines are oily fish, which offer a great source of health-giving omega-3 essential fatty acids. You should aim to eat oily fish at least once a week to ensure that you consume an adequate amount of this valuable nutrient.

Mango and shrimp curry

Rich and full-flavored, this spicy curry from Goa offers the perfect balance of sweet and sharp, spicy and creamy, and smooth and chunky. The green mango, used here as a vegetable, gives the curry a great texture.

INGREDIENTS *1 teaspoon chili powder* ‖ *1 teaspoon paprika* ‖ *½ teaspoon turmeric* ‖ *3 garlic cloves, crushed* ‖ *2 teaspoons finely grated fresh ginger root* ‖ *2 tablespoons ground coriander* ‖ *2 teaspoons ground cumin* ‖ *1 tablespoon grated jaggery or palm sugar* ‖ *1¾ cups water* ‖ *1 green mango, stoned and thinly sliced* ‖ *1¾ cups low-fat coconut milk* ‖ *1 tablespoon tamarind paste* ‖ *2 pounds raw jumbo shrimp, cleaned and deveined* ‖ *salt*

ONE Put the chili powder, paprika, turmeric, garlic, ginger, ground coriander, cumin, and jaggery into a large wok with the water and stir to mix well. Place over high heat and bring the mixture to a boil. Reduce the heat and cook covered for 8–10 minutes. **TWO** Add the mango, coconut milk, and tamarind paste and stir to combine. Bring the mixture back to a boil and add the shrimp. **THREE** Stir and cook gently for 8–10 minutes or until all the shrimp have turned pink and are cooked through. Season and serve the curry with steamed basmati rice.

Serves 4

NUTRIENT ANALYSIS PER SERVING 255 cal – 1070 kJ – 24 g protein – 18 g carbohydrates – 14 g sugars – 10 g fat – 6 g saturated fat – 1 g fiber – 372 mg sodium

HEALTHY TIP Although shrimp contain cholesterol, saturated fats are the real villain. The liver turns saturated fats into cholesterol in the body, thus raising your overall cholesterol levels. Shrimp are low in saturated fat and have many other health benefits, so most health professionals agree that it's fine to eat them, even if you're trying to reduce your cholesterol levels.

Bombay-style fish

Fish cooked simply in a rich spice paste makes a quick and tasty lunch or dinner dish. Serve with light, fresh vegetable side dishes and plain steamed or boiled rice to offer a good balance of contrasting textures and flavors.

INGREDIENTS *1 teaspoon cardamom seeds* ‖ *1 teaspoon fennel seeds* ‖ *2 teaspoons coriander seeds* ‖ *1 teaspoon cumin seeds* ‖ *2 strands mace* ‖ *1 teaspoon white poppy seeds* ‖ *½ cup cashews, roasted and chopped* ‖ *3 tablespoons dried coconut* ‖ *1 red onion, finely chopped* ‖ *3 garlic cloves, chopped* ‖ *2 jalapeños, seeded and chopped* ‖ *large handful of chopped cilantro leaves* ‖ *2 tablespoons chopped mint leaves* ‖ *juice of 2 limes* ‖ *1 tablespoon sunflower oil* ‖ *1 scant cup water* ‖ *1 large pomfret, cleaned and cut into 4 thick steaks or 4 thick 7-ounce cod fillets* ‖ *red chillies, finely chopped, to garnish*

ONE In a small frying pan, dry-roast the cardamom seeds, fennel seeds, coriander seeds, cumin seeds, and mace for a few minutes over medium heat until aromatic. Remove from heat and transfer to a coffee grinder; add the poppy seeds and grind to a fine powder. **TWO** Place the cashews and coconut in a frying pan and roast for a few minutes over medium heat until the coconut is lightly colored. Transfer to a food processor with the spice mix, red onion, garlic, jalapeño, cilantro leaves, mint leaves, and the lime juice. Blend to form a paste. **THREE** Heat the oil in a large, nonstick frying pan and add the spice paste. Stir and fry for 1–2 minutes over high heat and then add the water. Stir to mix well, bring to a boil, and then gently lay the fish fillets across the bottom of the pan. **FOUR** Reduce the heat to medium and simmer gently for 8–10 minutes or until the fish is cooked through. Garnish with finely chopped red chiles and serve immediately with pappadams, other crackers, or basmati rice.

Serves 4

NUTRIENT ANALYSIS PER SERVING 353 cal – 1475 kJ – 40 g protein – 8 g carbohydrates – 4 g sugars – 19 g fat – 7 g saturated fat – 3 g fiber – 164 mg sodium

HEALTHY TIP Dry-roasting the spices, cashews and coconut in a clean frying pan helps to bring out their flavor, without adding extra fat.

Baked halibut masala

Nothing could be simpler than coating halibut steaks or fillets in a ready-made curry paste mixed with lime juice, then baking them until just cooked through. They're so delicious that all you need is a bowl of steamed rice and a simple vegetable side dish to make a well-balanced meal.

INGREDIENTS *4 thick halibut steaks or fillets, each about 8 ounces* ‖ *2 tablespoons medium curry paste* ‖ *juice of 2 limes*

ONE Line a large baking sheet with nonstick parchment paper. **TWO** Mix together the curry paste and lime juice. Season, and spread this mixture over the fish. **THREE** Put the fish on the prepared baking sheet and bake in a preheated oven, 400°F, for 15–20 minutes or until the fish is cooked through. Remove from the oven and serve immediately with steamed rice and vegetables.

Serves 4

NUTRIENT ANALYSIS PER SERVING 190 cal – 808 kJ – 32 g protein – 1 g carbohydrates – 1 g sugars – 7 g fat – 1 g saturated fat – 0 g fiber – 337 mg sodium

HEALTHY TIP Fish such as halibut offers an excellent source of low-fat protein, and preparing it as is done here—with a spicy marinade, then baking it in the oven—is one of the healthiest ways to enjoy it.

Tandoori fish kebabs

Dishes cooked in a tandoor clay oven have a very distinctive flavor. This version—using a classic yogurt-based marinade with traditional spices, and then the fish grilled until just cooked through—is equally good.

INGREDIENTS *4 trout fillets, each about 5 ounces, skinned*

TANDOORI MARINADE *1 cup low-fat plain yogurt* ‖ *3 garlic cloves, crushed* ‖ *1 teaspoon finely grated fresh ginger root* ‖ *1 tablespoon tandoori spice mix* ‖ *juice of 1 lemon* ‖ *salt*

ONE Trim the trout fillets and place them in a wide, nonreactive bowl in a single layer. Mix together all the ingredients for the marinade, season, and spread this mixture all over the fish. Cover and allow to marinate for 15–20 minutes if time permits. **TWO** Thread 2 presoaked bamboo skewers through each fillet and arrange them on a grill rack. Place under a preheated medium-hot broiler and cook for 4–5 minutes on each side or until cooked through. Remove from the grill rack and serve hot, with flatbreads and salad.

Serves 4

NUTRIENT ANALYSIS PER SERVING 207 cal – 870 kJ – 32 g protein – 5 g carbohydrates – 4 g sugars – 7 g fat – 0 g saturated fat – 0 g fiber – 128 mg sodium

HEALTHY TIP Although the consumption of fat should be restricted in a healthy diet, some fats, such as omega-3 fatty acids—a plentiful supply of which are found in trout—are essential for good health. They are believed to improve heart health, fight against cancer, and even improve the condition of your skin.

Salmon and tamarind curry

Tamarind adds a lovely sharp tang to this curry, and helps to cut through the richness of the salmon and coconut milk and enhance the flavors of the spices. It is available in most large supermarkets and Asian stores, but if you can't find it, you can use the juice of a lemon or lime instead.

INGREDIENTS *2 tablespoons sunflower oil* ‖ *2 garlic cloves, thinly sliced* ‖ *2 teaspoons cumin seeds* ‖ *1 teaspoon black onion seeds (nigella)* ‖ *1 teaspoon black mustard seeds* ‖ *1 teaspoon crushed coriander seeds* ‖ *10–12 curry leaves* ‖ *1½ pounds salmon fillet, cut into bite-sized pieces* ‖ *2 tablespoons tomato purée* ‖ *½ teaspoon sugar* ‖ *1 teaspoon garam masala* ‖ *1 teaspoon ground cumin* ‖ *6 tablespoons finely chopped cilantro leaves* ‖ *1 red chile, finely sliced* ‖ *1 teaspoon tamarind paste* ‖ *1 cup coconut milk* ‖ *salt* ‖ *pilau or steamed basmati rice, to serve*

TO GARNISH *cilantro leaves* ‖ *black onion seeds (nigella)*

ONE Heat the oil in a large, nonstick wok or frying pan. When it is hot, add the garlic, cumin seeds, black onion seeds, mustard seeds, and coriander seeds. Stir-fry for 1–2 minutes, then add the curry leaves and the salmon. Stir-fry over high heat for 5–6 minutes. **TWO** In a bowl, mix together the remaining ingredients and pour into the fish mixture. Turn the heat down to medium and let simmer for 3–4 minutes, stirring often, until the salmon pieces are cooked through. Season well and serve immediately, garnished with cilantro leaves and a few black onion seeds (nigella). Accompany with pilau or steamed basmati rice.

Serves 4

NUTRIENT ANALYSIS PER SERVING 628 cal – 2606 kJ – 37 g protein – 9 g carbohydrates – 7 g sugars – 50 g fat – 23 g saturated fat – 0 g fiber – 212 mg sodium

HEALTHY TIP Salmon is a rich source of essential fatty acids, which are necessary for good health and are believed to help protect against heart disease.

Masala fennel shrimp

Fresh, juicy shrimp, cooked simply in a fennel-spiced sauce, makes for a healthy lunch when served with rice and a chopped salad.

INGREDIENTS *1 teaspoon light olive oil* ‖ *10–12 fresh curry leaves* ‖ *2 large shallots, halved and finely sliced* ‖ *2 teaspoons finely grated garlic* ‖ *1 teaspoon finely grated fresh ginger root* ‖ *1 tablespoon fennel seeds* ‖ *1 tablespoon mild curry powder* ‖ *5 large, ripe tomatoes, seeded and chopped* ‖ *1½ pounds raw jumbo shrimp, peeled and deveined* ‖ *sea salt* ‖ *fresh cilantro leaves, to garnish*

ONE Heat the oil in a large wok or nonstick frying pan and add the curry leaves. Stir-fry for 30 seconds, and add the shallots. Stir-fry over medium heat for 4–5 minutes, then add the garlic, ginger, and fennel seeds. **TWO** Cook gently for 2–3 minutes, then add the curry powder and tomatoes. Turn the heat to high and stir-fry the mixture for 3–4 minutes. **THREE** Add the shrimp and cook over high heat for 6–7 minutes or until the shrimp turn pink and are just cooked through. Remove from heat, season, and garnish with fresh cilantro leaves. Serve immediately with steamed rice.

Serves 4

NUTRIENT ANALYSIS PER SERVING 142 cal – 599 kJ – 18 g protein – 8 g carbohydrates – 6 g sugars – 5 g fat – 1 g saturated fat – 3 g fiber – 202 mg sodium

HEALTHY TIP Stir-frying is a very healthy cooking technique, using minimum fat. Using a nonstick pan or wok means that you need even less fat to prevent the ingredients from sticking to the pan.

Creamy fish korma

Delicately flavored korma curries are usually enriched with cream and ground almonds, but here low-fat coconut milk and very low-fat fromage frais or yogurt are used instead. The final result is just as good and really makes the most of fresh cod.

INGREDIENTS *1½ pounds thick cod fillet, skinned and cut into bite-sized cubes* ‖ *2 tablespoons flour* ‖ *2 tablespoons light olive oil* ‖ *1 onion, halved and thinly sliced* ‖ *2 garlic cloves crushed* ‖ *1 teaspoon turmeric* ‖ *1 jalapeño, finely chopped* ‖ *2 tablespoons lemon juice* ‖ *1 cup low-fat coconut milk* ‖ *½ cup very low-fat plain fromage frais or low-fat plain yogurt*

ONE Lightly coat the fish with flour, patting away any excess. Heat the oil in a large, nonstick frying pan over medium heat and add the fish. Fry the fish for 2–3 minutes on each side. Remove from the pan with a slotted spoon and set aside. **TWO** Add the onion to the pan and stir-fry over medium heat for 5–6 minutes. Add the garlic, turmeric, jalapeño, and lemon juice and stir-fry for another 2–3 minutes. Stir in the coconut milk, bring to a boil, and then reduce the heat and stir and simmer gently for 8–10 minutes. **THREE** Return the fish to the pan, spoon the sauce over the fish, and cook for 4–5 minutes until heated through. Remove from the heat and gently stir in the fromage frais or yogurt before serving.

Serves 4

NUTRIENT ANALYSIS PER SERVING 315 cal – 1324 kJ – 39 g protein – 15 g carbohydrates – 6 g sugars – 12 g fat – 4 g saturated fat – 1 g fiber – 219 mg sodium

HEALTHY TIP To make a balanced, healthy meal, serve this rich curry with a simple, fresh vegetable side dish and plain steamed rice or warm chapatis.

Herbed spiced shrimp parcels

Steaming shrimp inside little foil parcels so that they cook lightly in their own juices is one of the healthiest ways of cooking them. Coating the shrimp first in a paste of coconut milk and spices gives them a rich, rounded flavor.

INGREDIENTS *1¾ pounds raw jumbo shrimp, cleaned and deveined*

HERBED SPICE PASTE *2 garlic cloves, finely chopped* ‖ *1 teaspoon finely grated fresh ginger root* ‖ *4 green onions, finely chopped* ‖ *6 tablespoons chopped fresh cilantro leaves* ‖ *1 cup low-fat coconut milk* ‖ *1 red chile, chopped* ‖ *1 teaspoon ground cumin* ‖ *½ teaspoon garam masala* ‖ *¼ teaspoon turmeric* ‖ *finely grated zest and juice of 1 lime* ‖ *1 teaspoon grated jaggery or palm sugar* ‖ *salt*

ONE Place the shrimp in a wide, shallow dish. **TWO** Put all the ingredients for the paste mixture into a food processor and blend until you have a coarse purée. Spoon this mixture over the shrimp and toss to coat them evenly. **THREE** Make 4 squares of doubled-sided foil 12 inches square and divide the shrimp mixture between them. To seal the shrimp in, make a parcel by bringing the edges of the foil together and crimping them together. **FOUR** Lay the parcels on a baking sheet and place it in a preheated oven, 400°F, and cook for 15–20 minutes or until the shrimp have turned pink and are cooked through. Remove the parcels from the oven, place each one on a plate, and serve immediately; open the parcels at the table.

Serves 4

NUTRIENT ANALYSIS PER SERVING 152 cal – 635 kJ – 19 g protein – 6 g carbohydrates – 4 g sugars – 6 g fat – 3 g saturated fat – 0 g fiber – 246 mg sodium

HEALTHY TIP Garlic, one of the essential flavorings in Indian cooking, has many health-giving properties. It's a natural antibacterial, and is also believed to help protect against certain forms of cancer and boost the immune system.

Goan-style clams and mussels

Goa, on the western shore of India, offers a rich source of inspiration for preparing fish and shellfish. Here, fresh clams and mussels are steamed with a rich blend of warm spices, then tossed with sweet grated coconut and fragrant cilantro make an utterly delicious dish.

INGREDIENTS *1 tablespoon sunflower oil ‖ 2 shallots, very finely sliced ‖ 1 red chile, slit lengthways ‖ 1 teaspoon finely grated fresh ginger root ‖ 2 garlic cloves, finely chopped ‖ 2 plum tomatoes, finely chopped ‖ 1 teaspoon garam masala ‖ ½ teaspoon turmeric ‖ 1¼ pounds fresh clams, scrubbed ‖ 2 pounds fresh mussels, scrubbed ‖ 7 ounces fresh grated coconut ‖ 6–8 tablespoons chopped cilantro leaves*

TO SERVE *lime or lemon wedges ‖ crusty bread*

ONE Heat the oil in a large wok or saucepan. Add the shallots, red chile, ginger, and garlic and stir-fry over high heat for 2–3 minutes. Add the tomatoes, garam masala, and turmeric and continue to cook for 3–4 minutes, stirring often. **TWO** Pour in the clams and mussels, stir to mix, and cover tightly. Continue to cook over high heat for 6–8 minutes or until the clams and mussels have opened. Discard any that remain closed. **THREE** Stir in the grated coconut and cilantro, and mix well. Serve in large individual bowls with lemon or lime wedges to squeeze over. Eat with your fingers and have plenty of crusty bread on hand to mop up any juices.

Serves 4

NUTRIENT ANALYSIS PER SERVING 304 cal – 1266 kJ – 20 g protein – 5 g carbohydrates – 4 g sugars – 23 g fat – 16 g saturated fat – 7 g fiber – 232 mg sodium

HEALTHY TIP Shellfish are a useful source of zinc, which plays an important role in the body's growth, immunity, and reproductive functions.

Vegetables
and vegetarian

Okra with tomato and cucumber

People are often nervous about cooking okra because of its slightly gluey texture, but it is simple to cook well, and once you have tried this tasty recipe, it is sure to become a regular dish in your repertoire.

INGREDIENTS *¾ pound fresh okra* ‖ *2 tablespoons sunflower oil* ‖ *2 tablespoons mustard seeds* ‖ *2 dried red chiles (whole)* ‖ *1 onion, very finely sliced* ‖ *2 plum tomatoes, roughly chopped* ‖ *1 small cucumber, roughly chopped* ‖ *1 garlic clove, very finely chopped* ‖ *1 teaspoon very finely chopped fresh ginger root* ‖ *½ teaspoon turmeric* ‖ *salt* ‖ *freshly grated coconut, to sprinkle*

ONE Slice the okra diagonally into ½-inch slices. Heat the oil in a large, nonstick frying pan; when hot, add the mustard seeds. As they begin to "pop," add the dried red chiles and onion. **TWO** Stir-fry and cook over medium heat for 4–5 minutes until the onion has softened, and then stir in the tomatoes, cucumber, garlic, ginger, and turmeric. Stir-fry for another 3–4 minutes and then turn the heat to high and add the sliced okra. Stir-fry for 2–3 minutes, season, and remove from heat. **THREE** Sprinkle with the grated coconut and serve immediately.

Serves 4

NUTRIENT ANALYSIS PER SERVING 149 cal – 617 kJ – 5 g protein – 10 g carbohydrates – 7 g sugars – 10 g fat – 3 g saturated fat – 6 g fiber – 17 mg sodium

HEALTHY TIP You should aim to eat five servings of fruit and vegetables a day, covering a good range of different types. Include this dish as part of a meal, and you'll be well on your way to your five a day.

Lime and cilantro potatoes with zucchini

Potatoes and zucchini are a classic combination in Indian cooking, and the addition of zingy lime juice and fragrant fresh herbs really sets them off. This dish is particularly good served with Indian breads for scooping up the spiced potatoes.

INGREDIENTS *1 tablespoon sunflower oil* ‖ *1 small onion, finely diced* ‖ *2 teaspoons cumin seeds* ‖ *2 garlic cloves, crushed* ‖ *1 teaspoon finely grated fresh root ginger* ‖ *½ teaspoon turmeric* ‖ *1¼ pounds potatoes, cut into thick matchsticks and boiled until soft* ‖ *½ cup hot water* ‖ *1 zucchini, cut into thick matchsticks and boiled* ‖ *2 plum tomatoes, finely chopped* ‖ *½ teaspoon garam masala* ‖ *¼ cup chopped fresh cilantro leaves* ‖ *2 tablespoons chopped fresh mint leaves* ‖ *juice and finely grated zest of 1 lime* ‖ *salt*

ONE Heat the oil in a large, nonstick wok or frying pan and add the onion. Stir-fry over medium heat for 5–6 minutes until softened. **TWO** Add the cumin seeds, garlic, ginger, and turmeric. Stir-fry for 2–3 minutes and then add the potatoes and the water. Cook over high heat for 3–4 minutes, then stir in the zucchini, tomatoes, and garam masala. Stir and cook on high for 3–4 minutes, remove from heat, and stir in the chopped herbs and the lime zest and juice. Season well and serve immediately.

Serves 4

NUTRIENT ANALYSIS PER SERVING 204 cal – 858 kJ – 8 g protein – 36 g carbohydrates – 4 g sugars – 5 g fat – 1 g saturated fat – 6 g fiber – 20 mg sodium

HEALTHY TIP Zucchini offer a good supply of folic acid, which is essential for the development of the fetus. Women in the first three months of pregnancy, or who are trying to become pregnant, should eat plenty of foods containing this valuable nutrient.

Green bean stir-fry with curry leaves
Fresh crunchy beans, cooked in spices until barely tender, then sprinkled with freshly grated coconut, make a delicious accompaniment to simply cooked meat and fish dishes.

INGREDIENTS *1 tablespoon sunflower oil* ‖ *1 teaspoon black mustard seeds* ‖ *10–12 curry leaves* ‖ *1 teaspoon urad dhal* ‖ *1–2 dried red chiles* ‖ *1 small onion, halved and thinly sliced* ‖ *1 teaspoon turmeric* ‖ *¾ pound fine green beans, trimmed* ‖ *½ cup water* ‖ *salt* ‖ *2 tablespoons freshly grated coconut*

ONE Heat the oil in a large, nonstick frying pan or wok. Add the mustard seeds and cook over medium heat. As soon as the seeds start to "pop," add the curry leaves, urad dhal, and dried red chiles. Stir-fry for 1–2 minutes or until the dhal turns lightly golden. **TWO** Add the onion, stir, and cook for 5–6 minutes until softened, then add the turmeric and continue to stir-fry for 2–3 minutes. **THREE** Add the beans to the pan with the water; stir, cover, and cook over medium-low heat for 5–6 minutes, stirring occasionally. Season well and remove from heat. Sprinkle with the coconut just before serving.

Serves 4

NUTRIENT ANALYSIS PER SERVING 93 cal – 387 kJ – 3 g protein – 7 g carbohydrates – 3 g sugars – 6 g fat – 2 g saturated fat – 4 g fiber – 4 mg sodium

HEALTHY TIP For maximum nutrition, buy beans in season and choose firm, crisp ones; avoid pretrimmed vegetables or any that are going soft.

Mixed vegetable and coconut stew

Rich and creamy, this terrific stew makes a great vegetarian main dish. The vegetables are cooked until only just tender, giving the stew a fresh, clean flavor and a good texture.

INGREDIENTS *2 carrots, cut into thin strips* ‖ *1 zucchini, cut into thin strips* ‖ *½ pound green beans, trimmed and cut in half* ‖ *1 medium potato, cut into thin strips* ‖ *1 tablespoon sunflower oil* ‖ *1 large onion, halved and thinly sliced* ‖ *½ teaspoon black mustard seeds* ‖ *6–8 curry leaves* ‖ *1 jalapeño, seeded and thinly sliced* ‖ *1 teaspoon poppy seeds* ‖ *1 cup coconut milk* ‖ *juice of half a lemon* ‖ *½ cup water* ‖ *salt* ‖ *chopped cilantro leaves, to garnish*

ONE Place the prepared vegetables in a bowl of cold water. **TWO** Heat the oil in a large, nonstick wok or frying pan; when the oil is hot add the onion. Stir and cook over medium heat for 4–5 minutes. Add the mustard seeds, curry leaves, and jalapeño and stir-fry for 2–3 minutes. **THREE** Drain the vegetables and add them to the pan with the poppy seeds, coconut milk, lemon juice, and the measured water. Season, and bring to a boil. Reduce the heat, cover, and cook gently for 6–7 minutes or until the vegetables are just tender. Stir in the chopped cilantro and serve immediately.

Serves 4

NUTRIENT ANALYSIS PER SERVING 188 kcal – 779 kJ – 4 g protein – 17 g carbohydrates – 9 g sugars – 12 g fat – 6 g saturated fat – 4 g fiber – 70 mg sodium

HEALTHY TIP The fresh, lightly cooked vegetables in this dish offer an excellent source of many important nutrients and will make a good contribution toward your recommended five daily servings.

Masala grilled tomatoes

These spicy tomatoes make a great accompaniment to meat and fish dishes, but they're also good served on toast as a satisfying snack.

INGREDIENTS *1½ pounds ripe, fresh plum tomatoes ‖ 1 teaspoon garam masala ‖ 1 teaspoon ground coriander ‖ 2 teaspoons cumin seeds ‖ ½ teaspoon chili powder ‖ juice of 1 lemon ‖ light olive oil to drizzle ‖ salt and freshly ground black pepper ‖ roughly chopped cilantro and mint leaves, to garnish*

ONE Cut the tomatoes in half lengthwise and lay them on a grill rack, cut side up. Sprinkle with the garam masala, ground coriander, cumin seeds, chili powder, and lemon juice. Lightly drizzle with the olive oil and season well. **TWO** Place under a preheated broiler turned on high, about 4 inches from the source of the heat, and grill for 5–6 minutes or until the tops are lightly browned and the tomatoes slightly limp. Remove from the rack and place on a serving plate. Sprinkle with the chopped herbs and serve.

Serves 4

NUTRIENT ANALYSIS PER SERVING 59 cal – 249 kJ – 2 g protein – 7 g carbohydrates – 6 g sugars – 3 g fat – 1 g saturated fat – 3 g fiber – 27 g sodium

HEALTHY TIP Tomatoes contain the valuable phytochemical lycopene, which is thought to protect against certain cancers. Cooked tomatoes appear to be a richer source of lycopene than when eaten fresh.

Cucumber and coconut curry

Mild-tasting cucumber is complemented perfectly by hot chiles, fragrant spices, tart tamarind, and rich, sweet coconut in this utterly delectable stir-fry. Serve as a vegetable accompaniment with meat, fish, or other vegetable dishes.

INGREDIENTS *1 tablespoon tamarind paste* ‖ *¼ cup water* ‖ *½ teaspoon fenugreek seeds* ‖ *2 dried red chiles* ‖ *3½ ounces freshly grated coconut* ‖ *½ teaspoon turmeric* ‖ *2 tablespoons sunflower oil* ‖ *1 tablespoon mustard seeds* ‖ *1 teaspoon cumin seeds* ‖ *8–10 curry leaves* ‖ *1 pound cucumber, cut into ½-inch cubes* ‖ *salt*

ONE Mix the tamarind paste with the water and set aside. **TWO** In a frying pan, dry-roast the fenugreek seeds and red chiles for 1 minute over a low heat. Transfer them to a mortar and pestle with the tamarind mixture, half the coconut, and the turmeric and pound to a coarse paste. **THREE** Heat the oil in a frying pan and when hot add the mustard seeds. As soon as they start to "pop," stir in the cumin seeds, curry leaves, and coconut mixture. Stir and cook over medium heat for 2–3 minutes and then add the cucumber. Continue to stir and cook for 5–6 minutes, season well, and sprinkle with the remaining coconut. Serve immediately.

Serves 4

NUTRIENT ANALYSIS PER SERVING 190 cal – 788 kJ – 3 g protein – 8 g carbohydrates – 5 g sugars – 16 g fat – 8 g saturated fat – 4 g fiber – 12 mg sodium

HEALTHY TIP Cucumber may seem an unusual vegetable to stir-fry, but it tastes delicious and also has several health benefits. Cucumbers are a natural diuretic and are also believed to help reduce high blood pressure.

Pea and potato bhaji

Bhaji is the word used to describe simple vegetable dishes and should not be confused with the deep-fried fritters known as *bhajiyas*. Here, peas are combined with diced potatoes and fragrant, warming spices in a simple, tasty stir-fry that is quick to cook and the perfect accompaniment to any main dish.

INGREDIENTS *1 tablespoon light olive oil* ‖ *2 teaspoons black mustard seeds* ‖ *1 tablespoon fresh ginger root, peeled and cut into fine strips* ‖ *2 teaspoons cumin seeds* ‖ *2 dried red chiles* ‖ *¾ pound fresh or frozen spring peas* ‖ *¾ pound potatoes, boiled and cut into ¾-inch cubes* ‖ *2–3 tablespoons water* ‖ *sea salt* ‖ *1 tablespoon freshly grated coconut, to garnish*

ONE Heat the oil in a large nonstick frying pan and when hot add the mustard seeds. Stir-fry for 2–3 minutes until they start to "pop," then add the ginger, cumin, red chile, peas, and potatoes. **TWO** Stir-fry over high heat for 3–4 minutes, add the water, cover, and reduce the heat to low. Cook gently for 2–3 minutes and remove from heat. Season and sprinkle with the coconut and serve with rotis or flatbreads.

Serves 4

NUTRIENT ANALYSIS PER SERVING 225 cal – 940 kJ – 11 g protein – 31 g carbohydrates – 3 g sugars – 7 g fat – 2 g saturated fat – 7 g fiber – 14 mg sodium

HEALTHY TIP Carbohydrates are an important part of any healthy, balanced diet, providing the body with energy. Dishes rich in carbohydrates, such as this potato one, should be combined with fresh vegetables and a protein dish, such as a fish or meat curry or dhal.

Broccoli with garlic, cumin, and red chile

Crisp, fresh broccoli is delicious stir-fried with garlic, chiles, and warm spices. The simple, clean flavors make this dish the perfect accompaniment to richer meat or fish dishes.

INGREDIENTS *1 tablespoon chickpea flour (besan or gram flour)* ‖ *1 teaspoon salt* ‖ *1 teaspoon ground cumin* ‖ *1 teaspoon ground coriander* ‖ *½ teaspoon garam masala* ‖ *2 tablespoons light olive oil* ‖ *4 garlic cloves, thinly sliced* ‖ *2 teaspoons cumin seeds* ‖ *2 red chiles, deseeded and sliced* ‖ *1¼ pounds broccoli florets* ‖ *1–2 tablespoons water*

ONE In a small bowl mix together the chickpea flour, salt, ground cumin, ground coriander, and garam masala. **TWO** Heat the oil in a large, nonstick wok or frying pan; when it is hot add the garlic, cumin seeds and chiles and stir-fry for 1–2 minutes. **THREE** Add the broccoli and stir-fry over high heat for 3–4 minutes. Reduce the heat to low and evenly sprinkle the chickpea flour mixture over the broccoli. Cover the pan and cook gently for 5-6 minutes. **FOUR** Take the lid off the pan and sprinkle the water over the broccoli; stir and cook until the florets are evenly coated with the mixture. Check the seasoning and serve immediately.

Serves 4

NUTRIENT ANALYSIS PER SERVING 134 cal – 557 kJ – 9 g protein – 7 g carbohydrates – 2 g sugars – 8 g fat – 1 g saturated fat – 1 g fiber – 505 mg sodium

HEALTHY TIP Broccoli is a good source of vitamin C, folic acid, iron, and potassium and is also believed to have cancer-fighting properties. Cooking it lightly in this way destroys fewer of its natural nutrients than boiling.

Spinach, red pepper, and chickpea bhaji

This simple vegetable dish is best served with dhal and chapatis to make a complete vegetarian meal. The chickpeas provide a valuable source of protein in the vegetarian diet.

INGREDIENTS *1 tablespoon sunflower oil* ‖ *1 teaspoon finely grated fresh ginger root* ‖ *2 garlic cloves, crushed* ‖ *1 large shallot, finely chopped* ‖ *1 red bell pepper, deseeded and cut into thin strips* ‖ *1 teaspoon chili powder* ‖ *1 teaspoon ground cumin* ‖ *1 teaspoon ground coriander* ‖ *2 tablespoons tomato purée* ‖ *1 cup water* ‖ *13 ounces baby spinach leaves* ‖ *1 x 13-ounce can chickpeas, drained* ‖ *salt*

ONE Heat the oil in a large nonstick frying pan. Add the ginger and garlic and stir-fry for 30 seconds over medium heat. Add the shallot and red bell pepper; stir and cook for 5–6 minutes until slightly softened. **TWO** Stir in the chili powder, ground cumin, ground coriander, and tomato purée. Stir-fry for 2–3 minutes, then pour in the water, stir, and bring to a boil. Stir in the spinach and chickpeas and cook for 5–6 minutes until the spinach has just wilted. Season and serve immediately.

Serves 4

NUTRIENT ANALYSIS PER SERVING 177 cal – 743 kJ – 11 g protein – 21 g carbohydrates – 6 g sugars – 6 g fat – 1 g saturated fat – 9 g fiber – 185 mg sodium

HEALTHY TIP Try to find chickpeas canned in water, rather than brine, because the brined variety tend to be fairly high in salt. If you can only find chickpeas in brine, rinse them really well in cold running water before adding them to the dish.

Tomato egg curry

Whole boiled eggs cooked in a spicy sauce is a popular dish throughout India. Serve them with simple steamed rice or flatbreads and a vegetable side or salad for a healthy, nutritious meal.

INGREDIENTS *1 tablespoon sunflower oil* ‖ *1 large onion, halved and thinly sliced* ‖ *1 teaspoon finely grated fresh ginger root* ‖ *2 garlic cloves, crushed* ‖ *2 tablespoons medium curry powder* ‖ *1 x 14-ounce can diced tomatoes* ‖ *1 teaspoon honey or sugar* ‖ *8 large eggs, hard-boiled, peeled, and halved* ‖ *salt* ‖ *¼ cup low-fat yogurt, to drizzle over*

TO GARNISH *chopped cilantro leaves* ‖ *roasted cumin seeds*

ONE Heat the oil in a large, nonstick frying pan and add the onion. Cook over medium heat for 10–12 minutes until softened and lightly golden. Add the ginger, garlic, and curry powder, and stir and cook for 1 minute. **TWO** Stir in the chopped tomatoes and sugar, bring the mixture to a boil, reduce the heat, cover, and cook gently for 10–12 minutes, stirring often. Carefully add the eggs to the mixture and heat through gently until warmed. Drizzle with the yogurt, sprinkle with the coriander and cumin seeds, season, and serve immediately with steamed rice or warmed flatbread.

Serves 4

NUTRIENT ANALYSIS PER SERVING 300 cal – 1252 kJ – 21 g protein – 14 g carbohydrate – 11 g sugars – 18 g fat – 5 g saturates – 3 g fiber – 284 mg sodium

HEALTHY TIP Eggs are an excellent vegetarian source of protein, but they are also high in cholesterol, so anyone on a low-cholesterol diet should be careful not to eat too many eggs per week.

Indian masala omelet

Perfect for a lazy weekend breakfast or brunch, this hot and spicy omelet is a meal in itself. It's also great served with salad for a light lunch or supper.

INGREDIENTS *1 teaspoon sunflower oil* ‖ *½ small red onion, very finely diced* ‖ *1 plum tomato, seeded and very finely diced* ‖ *1 jalapeño, deseeded and thinly sliced* ‖ *pinch of turmeric* ‖ *½ teaspoon cumin seeds* ‖ *2 tablespoons chopped cilantro leaves* ‖ *2 large eggs, lightly beaten* ‖ *½ teaspoon salt*

ONE Heat the oil in a medium, nonstick frying pan. Mix together all the ingredients and pour into the pan. Cook over medium heat for 3–4 minutes, or until the base of the omelet is lightly browned. With a spatula, carefully fold over the omelet, press it down lightly with the spatula and cook for 2–3 minutes. Flip over the omelet and cook for another 2–3 minutes or until it is cooked to your liking. **TWO** Remove from heat and serve immediately with warm crusty bread or roll it up in a warm chapati.

Serves 1

NUTRIENT ANALYSIS PER SERVING 234 cal – 972 kJ – 16 g protein – 6 g carbohydrates – 4 g sugars – 16 g fat – 4 g saturated fat – 1 g fiber – 175 mg sodium

HEALTHY TIP Hot peppers are thought to boost the immune system and are often recommended for warding off colds and fevers.

Mustard-braised spiced cabbage

Mustard seeds cooked in hot oil until they "pop," have a sweet, nutty taste, and are a classic flavoring for many Indian vegetable dishes. They work well here combined with lightly cooked, sweet, and tender cabbage.

INGREDIENTS *1 tablespoon sunflower oil* ‖ *1½ tablespoons black mustard seeds* ‖ *10–12 fresh curry leaves* ‖ *1 teaspoon dried urad dhal* ‖ *2 onions, halved and very thinly sliced* ‖ *2 dried red chiles* ‖ *1 teaspoon turmeric* ‖ *1 pound green or white cabbage, very finely shredded* ‖ *½ cup water* ‖ *salt* ‖ *freshly grated coconut, to garnish*

ONE Heat the oil in a large, nonstick frying pan over medium heat. Add the mustard seeds; when they start to "pop," add the curry leaves and urad dhal. Stir-fry for 2–3 minutes or until the dhal starts to brown. **TWO** Stir in the onions and red chiles. Cook over high heat, stirring often, for 4–5 minutes or until the onions soften. Add the turmeric and the cabbage and stir and cook for 2–3 minutes. Add the water, cover, and cook gently for 5–7 minutes or until the cabbage has softened but still retains a crunch. Season and serve immediately, sprinkled with freshly grated coconut.

Serves 4

NUTRIENT ANALYSIS PER SERVING 148 cal – 616 kJ – 6 g protein – 15 g carbohydrates – 9 g sugars – 7 g fat – 2 g saturated fat – 6 g fiber – 14 mg sodium

HEALTHY TIP Cabbage is a member of the brassica family, which contains a rich supply of health-giving nutrients, including those that are believed to help protect against cancer. Green cabbage has more potent health-giving properties than white, but white cabbage gives particularly delicious, sweet, crisp results.

Indian-style mashed potatoes

There is something infinitely comforting about mashed potatoes, and this version, spiced with chiles and pepped up with lemon juice, is no exception. Serve as an accompaniment to grilled or baked meat or fish dishes, along with a light, fresh vegetable dish.

INGREDIENTS *2 pounds floury potatoes, roughly chopped ‖ 1 cup low-fat crème fraîche or low-fat sour cream ‖ 1 red chile, deseeded and finely sliced ‖ 6 tablespoons finely chopped cilantro leaves ‖ 4 green onions, finely sliced ‖ a pinch of chili powder ‖ juice of ½ lemon ‖ salt*

ONE Boil the potatoes in a large pan of lightly salted water for 12–15 minutes or until tender. Drain and mash with a potato masher or ricer; return the resulting mash back to the pan. **TWO** Stir in the crème fraîche or sour cream and mix with a wooden spoon until smooth and creamy, then add the red chile, chopped cilantro, green onions, chili powder, and lemon juice. Season well and serve.

Serves 4

NUTRIENT ANALYSIS PER SERVING 284 cal – 1194 kJ – 8 g protein – 47 g carbohydrates – 4 g sugars – 8 g fat – 5 g saturated fat – 4 g fiber – 77 mg sodium

HEALTHY TIP Crème fraîche adds a lovely rich creaminess to these mashed potatoes and makes a healthier alternative to the butter that is often added. Low-fat crème fraîche is widely available in most supermarkets and is a much better option than the full-fat variety. If you can't find crème fraîche, substitute sour cream.

Cauliflower tarka

Tarka is a seasoning technique unique to India. Spices are cooked in very hot oil to release their flavor, then the oil is used to season the food. Here, cauliflower is cooked in the flavored oil until just tender, making a delicious vegetable dish.

INGREDIENTS *1 tablespoon sunflower oil* ‖ *1 teaspoon cumin seeds* ‖ *1 teaspoon yellow mustard seeds* ‖ *1 pound cauliflower florets* ‖ *2 garlic cloves, finely chopped* ‖ *1-inch piece of fresh ginger root, cut into fine shreds* ‖ *2 red chiles, sliced* ‖ *½ teaspoon garam masala* ‖ *1 cup hot water* ‖ *salt and freshly ground black pepper*

ONE Heat the oil in a large nonstick wok or frying pan over medium heat. Add the cumin and mustard seeds. Stir-fry for 1 minute, then add the cauliflower, garlic, ginger, and red chiles. **TWO** Turn the heat to high and stir-fry for 6–7 minutes until the cauliflower is lightly browned at the edges. Stir in the garam masala along with the water, stir to mix well, cover, and cook on high for 1–2 minutes. Remove from heat, season, and serve immediately.

Serves 4

NUTRIENT ANALYSIS PER SERVING 86 cal – 359 kJ – 6 g protein – 6 g carbohydrate – 3 g sugars – 5 g fat – 1 g saturated fat – 2 g fiber – 15 mg sodium

HEALTHY TIP Cauliflower is a member of the brassica family, which contains valuable phytochemicals; it is believed that those can help prevent and fight against cancer.

Pumpkin curry

When cooked, pumpkin becomes sweet and makes the perfect partner for fiery chilli and warm spices such as cumin and turmeric. Despite its quick cooking time, this dish has a rounded flavor. Serve as a vegetable aside to meat and fish dishes or by itself with steamed basmati rice or flatbreads and maybe an accompanying salad.

INGREDIENTS *1 pound pumpkin or butternut squash, cut into 1-inch cubes* ‖ *1 teaspoon turmeric* ‖ *1 teaspoon smoked paprika* ‖ *2½ cups water* ‖ *7 ounces freshly grated coconut* ‖ *1 teaspoon cumin seeds* ‖ *1 tablespoon sunflower oil* ‖ *1 teaspoon black mustard seeds* ‖ *8–10 curry leaves* ‖ *2 small red chiles, split in half lengthways* ‖ *salt*

ONE Put the pumpkin or butternut squash in a saucepan with the turmeric, smoked paprika, and the water. Bring to a boil and simmer gently for 6–8 minutes or until tender. **TWO** Grind half of the coconut in a spice mill or a mortar and pestle with the cumin seeds. Stir this into the pumpkin mixture and stir and cook for 2–3 minutes. Remove from heat. **THREE** In a small, nonstick frying pan, heat the oil until hot and add the mustard seeds, curry leaves, and red chiles. Stir and cook over high heat for 1–2 minutes, then pour this mixture over the pumpkin curry. Season and serve.

Serves 4

NUTRIENT ANALYSIS PER SERVING 236 cal – 976 kJ – 3 g protein – 7 g carbohydrates – 4 g sugars – 22 g fat – 16 g saturated fat – 7 g fiber – 12 mg sodium

HEALTHY TIP Orange-fleshed vegetables such as pumpkins, carrots, and butternut squash are an excellent source of the immune-boosting nutrient betacarotene, which is said to help protect against heart disease and cancer.

Grains, rices, legumes, and breads

Spiced lemon rice

A typical southern Indian favorite, this citrus-flavored rice dish is a perfect side dish for plain grilled fish or chicken.

INGREDIENTS *1 cup basmati rice* | *1 tablespoon light olive oil* | *12–14 fresh curry leaves* | *1 dried red chile* | *1-inch piece of cassia bark or cinnamon stick* | *2 or 3 cloves* | *4–6 cardamom pods* | *2 teaspoons cumin seeds* | *¼ teaspoon turmeric* | *juice of 1 large lemon* | *1½ cups boiling water* | *sea salt* | *chopped cilantro leaves, to garnish*

ONE Place the rice in a strainer and wash it thoroughly under cold running water. Drain well and set aside. **TWO** Heat the oil in a nonstick saucepan; when it is hot, add the curry leaves, chile, cassia or cinnamon, cloves, cardamom, cumin seeds, and turmeric. Stir-fry for 20–30 seconds and add the rice. Stir-fry for 2 minutes, then add the lemon juice and the boiling water. Bring to a boil, cover the pan tightly, and reduce heat to low. **THREE** Cook for 10–12 minutes, remove from heat, and allow to stand undisturbed for 10 minutes. Fluff the rice with a fork, season, and garnish with the chopped cilantro before serving.

Serves 4

NUTRIENT ANALYSIS PER SERVING 240 cal – 1009 kJ – 5 g protein – 46 g carbohydrates – 0 g sugars – 4 g fat – 1 g saturated fat – 0 g fiber – 4 mg sodium

HEALTHY TIP Lemons are an excellent source of vitamin C, which is important for boosting the immune system, healing wounds, and protecting against heart disease. Vitamin C also helps the body absorb iron.

Brinjal and cashew rice

Brinjal is the Indian name for eggplant, which is enjoyed in a great many ways in Indian cooking. Here, the chunks of moist, juicy eggplant are in perfect contrast with the fluffy rice and rich, tender cashews.

INGREDIENTS *1⅓ cups basmati rice* ‖ *2 tablespoons sunflower oil* ‖ *4 shallots, thinly sliced* ‖ *1 teaspoon black mustard seeds* ‖ *2 dried red chiles* ‖ *6–8 curry leaves* ‖ *1-inch piece of cassia bark or cinnamon stick* ‖ *2–3 cardamom pods* ‖ *1 bay leaf* ‖ *½ pound eggplant, cut into bite-sized cubes* ‖ *1 teaspoon turmeric* ‖ *2 cups boiling water* ‖ *salt*

TO SERVE *juice of ½ lemon* ‖ *½ pound roasted red bell peppers, diced* ‖ *½ cup roasted cashews* ‖ *chopped fresh cilantro leaves*

ONE Rinse the rice in cold water several times, drain, and set aside. **TWO** Heat the oil in a large, nonstick wok or frying pan and when it is hot add the shallots, mustard seeds, dried red chiles, curry leaves, cassia or cinnamon, cardamom, and bay leaf. Stir and fry for 1–2 minutes, then add the drained rice. Stir gently to coat the rice with the spice mixture, then add the eggplant and turmeric. Stir to mix well and add to the boiling water. Season well and bring to a boil. Cover tightly, reduce the heat to low, and cook gently for 12–15 minutes. Remove from heat and let stand, covered and undisturbed for another 10 minutes. Add the lemon juice and red pepper, fluff the grains of rice with a fork, and sprinkle with the cashews and fresh cilantro. Serve immediately.

Serves 4

NUTRIENT ANALYSIS PER SERVING 426 cal – 1778 kJ – 9 g protein – 67 g carbohydrates – 3 g sugars – 12 g fat – 1 g saturated fat – 2 g fiber – 6 mg sodium

HEALTHY TIP Cashews not only add texture and flavor to this dish, but also provide protein and are a good source of the B vitamins.

Yogurt and herb rice

Lightly spiced rice tossed with fresh herbs and yogurt makes a tasty alternative to plain boiled or steamed rice. Yogurt is naturally cooling, so this dish makes a great accompaniment to really hot and spicy curries.

INGREDIENTS *3 cups basmati rice* ‖ *1 tablespoon sunflower oil* ‖ *1 teaspoon cumin seeds* ‖ *½ teaspoon crushed coriander seeds* ‖ *1 teaspoon black mustard seeds* ‖ *1 red chile* ‖ *½ teaspoon grated fresh ginger root* ‖ *3 cups very low-fat plain yogurt* ‖ *½ cup chopped fresh dill* ‖ *salt* ‖ *chopped red chiles, to garnish*

ONE Cook the rice according to the package directions until just tender, drain, and set aside. **TWO** Heat the oil in a large, nonstick frying pan and when it is hot add the cumin seeds, coriander seeds, and mustard seeds. As the seeds begin to "pop," add the chile and ginger, stir-fry for a few seconds, and then pour this mixture over the rice and stir to coat evenly. **THREE** Whisk the yogurt until smooth and stir it into the spiced rice with the chopped dill. Season and serve immediately with chopped red chiles to garnish.

Serves 4

NUTRIENT ANALYSIS PER SERVING 692 cal – 2898 kJ – 22 g protein – 136 g carbohydrates – 15 g sugars – 6 g fat – 1 g saturated fat – 0 g fiber – 170 g sodium

HEALTHY TIP The addition of yogurt gives this rice a deep richness, but with only a fraction of the fat of a rich, buttery rice dish such as pulao rice.

Minted rice with tomato and sprouted beans

The bean sprouts in this light and fresh stir-fried rice dish give it a crunchy bite, while the generous addition of garlic gives a rich, aromatic flavor.

INGREDIENTS *2 tablespoons light olive oil* ‖ *6 green onions, very finely sliced* ‖ *2 garlic cloves, finely chopped* ‖ *3 cups cooked, cooled Basmati rice* ‖ *2 ripe plum tomatoes, finely chopped* ‖ *8 ounces mixed sprouted beans (a mixture of aduki, mung, lentil, and chickpea sprouts)* ‖ *a small handful of mint leaves* ‖ *salt and freshly ground black pepper*

ONE Heat the oil in a large, nonstick wok or frying pan. When it is hot, add the green onions and garlic and stir-fry for 2–3 minutes. **TWO** Add the cooked rice and continue to stir-fry over high heat for 3–4 minutes. Stir in the tomatoes and mixed sprouted beans and continue to cook over high heat for 2–3 minutes or until warmed through. **THREE** Remove from the heat, season, and stir in the chopped mint leaves. Serve immediately.

Serves 4

NUTRIENT ANALYSIS PER SERVING 296 cal – 1250 kJ – 6 g protein – 56 g carbohydrates – 3 g sugars – 7 g fat – 1 g saturated fat – 6 g fiber – 12 mg sodium

HEALTHY TIP Sprouted beans are a living food, packed with valuable vitamins, minerals, and health-giving phytochemicals. They are widely available in large supermarkets and health food stores, or you can sprout your own at home.

Spiced vegetable semolina

This hearty dish, known as *uppama*, is rather like a pilaf. It comes from the southwestern state of Kerala, where there are many variations using different combinations of spices and vegetables. Mustard seeds are a traditional flavoring.

INGREDIENTS *¾ cup coarse semolina* ‖ *1 tablespoon sunflower oil* ‖ *1 teaspoon black mustard seeds* ‖ *1 teaspoon cumin seeds* ‖ *1 dried red chile* ‖ *10–12 curry leaves* ‖ *1 onion, finely chopped* ‖ *1 teaspoon garam masala* ‖ *1 carrot, finely diced* ‖ *1 cup fresh peas* ‖ *10–12 cherry tomatoes, halved* ‖ *2 cups boiling water* ‖ *salt* ‖ *freshly chopped cilantro leaves, to garnish* ‖ *lemon wedges, to serve*

ONE Place the semolina in a large, nonstick frying pan and dry-roast it over medium heat for 8–10 minutes or until golden brown. Remove from the pan and set aside. **TWO** Return the pan to the heat and add the oil. When it is hot, add the mustard seeds, cumin seeds, chile, curry leaves, and onion. Stir-fry over medium heat for 5–6 minutes or until the onion has softened, then add the garam masala, carrot, peas, and cherry tomatoes. Stir-fry for 1–2 minutes, add the semolina and the boiling water. Stir and cook for 5–6 minutes over low heat, until the semolina has absorbed all the water. Season, and garnish with chopped cilantro before serving with wedges of lemon.

Serves 4

NUTRIENT ANALYSIS PER SERVING 243 cal – 1024 kJ – 8 g protein – 44 g carbohydrates – 6 g sugars – 5 g fat – 1 g saturated fat – 4 g fiber – 19 mg sodium

HEALTHY TIP Starchy carbohydrates, such as the semolina used here, should form a part of every meal. They provide the body with energy to help keep you going throughout the day.

Chicken and mushroom pulao
Tasty and sustaining, this richly flavored rice dish can be served as a meal in itself or with a light, crunchy salad and, perhaps, some Date, Apricot, and Raisin Chutney (*see page 124*).

INGREDIENTS *1 tablespoon sunflower oil* ‖ *1 onion, finely diced* ‖ *1 teaspoon finely grated fresh ginger root* ‖ *1 teaspoon finely grated garlic* ‖ *2 teaspoons ground cumin* ‖ *½ teaspoon crushed cardamom seeds* ‖ *1-inch piece of cassia bark or cinnamon stick* ‖ *4 cloves* ‖ *½ pound skinless, boneless chicken thighs, cut into bite-sized pieces* ‖ *7 ounces shiitake mushrooms, thickly sliced* ‖ *1¼ pounds green beans, cut into 1-inch lengths* ‖ *2 cups fresh chicken stock* ‖ *1½ cups basmati rice, washed and drained* ‖ *salt and freshly ground black pepper*

ONE Heat the oil in a large, heavy-bottomed frying pan and add the onion. Cook over medium heat for 10–12 minutes or until softened and lightly browned. Add the ginger, garlic, cumin, cardamom, cassia bark or cinnamon stick, and cloves. Stir-fry for 2–3 minutes, then add the chicken and cook over high heat for 5–6 minutes. **TWO** Stir in the mushrooms, green beans, stock, and rice, season, and bring to a boil. Cover tightly, turn the heat to low, and cook gently for 12–15 minutes. Remove from heat and allow to stand uncovered and undisturbed for another 10 minutes. Fluff the grains of the rice with a fork and serve warm.

Serves 4

NUTRIENT ANALYSIS PER SERVING 403 cal – 1685 kJ – 20 g protein – 63 g carbohydrates – 2 g sugars – 8 g fat – 2 g saturated fat – 2 g fiber – 306 mg sodium

HEALTHY TIP A classic pulao often uses a generous quantity of oil, but this modern version uses only a little oil to fry the spices and aromatics and release their flavors. Using skinless chicken will further reduce the fat content of the dish.

Rice with dill

Studded with vibrant green peas, this extremely fragrant rice dish, infused with the warm sweetness of cardamom, cinnamon, and garam masala, makes a perfect side for any dish.

INGREDIENTS *2 cups basmati rice ‖ 1 tablespoon sunflower oil ‖ 3 cloves ‖ 6 cardamom pods, roughly crushed ‖ 1-inch piece of cassia bark or cinnamon stick ‖ 4 shallots, thinly sliced ‖ 1 teaspoon garam masala ‖ 6 tablespoons finely chopped fresh dill ‖ 1 cup fresh or frozen peas ‖ 2 cups water ‖ salt and freshly ground black pepper*

ONE Rinse the rice under cold water several times, drain, and set aside. **TWO** Heat the oil in a heavy-bottomed, nonstick saucepan over medium heat and add the cloves, cardamom, and cassia bark or cinnamon stick. Stir-fry for a few seconds, then add the shallots. Turn the heat to low and cook the shallots for 12–15 minutes until lightly browned, stirring often. **THREE** Add the drained rice to the saucepan with the garam masala, dill, and peas. Add the water, season, and bring the mixture to a boil. Cover the saucepan tightly, reduce the heat to low, and cook undisturbed for 15–20 minutes. Remove from heat, but do not uncover. Allow to stand for another 10–15 minutes. Fluff the rice before serving.

Serves 4

NUTRIENT ANALYSIS PER SERVING 435 cal – 1815 kJ – 11 g protein – 87 g carbohydrates – 2 g sugars – 4 g fat – 1 g saturated fat – 3 g fiber – 3 mg sodium

HEALTHY TIP In herbal medicine, dill is said to aid digestion and to have calming properties—making this rice dish the perfect accompaniment to a spicy, hot meal.

Chickpea curry
Chickpeas are an ancient food, eaten for millennia, and are a popular ingredient in Indian cooking. This classic curry uses canned chickpeas, so it takes virtually no time to cook and is perfect served as a vegetarian main dish or as one of several vegetable dishes.

INGREDIENTS *1 tablespoon sunflower oil* ‖ *2 garlic cloves, crushed* ‖ *1 teaspoon finely grated fresh ginger root* ‖ *2 tablespoons medium or hot curry powder* ‖ *1 x 13-ounce can diced tomatoes* ‖ *1 teaspoon grated jaggery or palm sugar* ‖ *2 x 13-ounce cans chickpeas, rinsed and drained* ‖ *salt* ‖ *low-fat yogurt, to drizzle* ‖ *small handful of chopped cilantro leaves, to garnish*

ONE Heat the oil in a large, nonstick wok or frying pan and add the garlic and ginger. Stir-fry for 30 seconds and add the curry powder. Stir and cook for 1 minute before adding the diced tomatoes and jaggery or palm sugar. Bring the mixture to a boil, cover, reduce the heat, and cook over medium heat for 10–12 minutes. **TWO** Stir in the chickpeas and mix well. Cook over medium heat for 3–4 minutes. Season, remove from heat. Drizzle with the low-fat yogurt and sprinkle with the chopped cilantro before serving.

Serves 4

NUTRIENT ANALYSIS PER SERVING 292 cal – 1232 kJ – 16 g protein – 39 g carbohydrates – 5 g sugars – 9 g fat – 1 g saturated fat – 1 g fiber – 503 mg sodium

HEALTHY TIP Legumes such as chickpeas contain useful amounts of various nutrients, including B vitamins, iron, calcium, and fiber. They are also a good source of complex carbohydrates, which are absorbed slowly into the body, providing a steady stream of energy.

Minted green mung bean curry

A large proportion of India's Hindu population are vegetarian, so beans and lentils make up an important part of the diet. The addition of coconut milk gives this spicy, wholesome curry a delicious richness, while the generous quantity of herbs gives it a fresh taste and aroma.

INGREDIENTS *½ pound green mung beans* ‖ *1 teaspoon chili powder* ‖ *½ teaspoon turmeric* ‖ *2½ cups water* ‖ *2 potatoes, diced* ‖ *½ cup low-fat coconut milk* ‖ *2 plum tomatoes, roughly chopped* ‖ *1 jalapeño, deseeded and finely chopped* ‖ *1–2 teaspoons grated palm sugar* ‖ *small handful roughly chopped mint leaves and cilantro leaves* ‖ *salt*

ONE Place the mung beans, chili powder and turmeric in a large saucepan with the water. Bring to a boil, cover, reduce the heat, and cook gently for 20–25 minutes. Add the potatoes and continue to cook for 12–15 minutes or until tender. **TWO** Stir in the coconut milk, tomatoes, and jalapeño and cook gently for 4–5 minutes. Stir in the palm sugar and cook for 2–3 minutes until dissolved. **THREE** Remove from heat, stir in the chopped herbs, season, and serve immediately.

Serves 4

NUTRIENT ANALYSIS PER SERVING 278 cal – 1180 kJ – 17 g protein – 46 g carbohydrates – 7 g sugars – 4 g fat – 2 g saturated fat – 10 g fiber – 68 mg sodium

HEALTHY TIP Pale green mung beans are an excellent source of protein, and they also offer a valuable source of fiber, which is essential for good digestion.

Spinach dhal

No Indian meal is complete without a bowl of spicy lentil dhal, which is one of the staple dishes eaten throughout the country. This version is flecked with fresh, tender baby spinach for extra flavor, color, and texture.

INGREDIENTS *8 ounces red lentils, rinsed and drained* ‖ *4 cups water* ‖ *¼ teaspoon turmeric* ‖ *1 teaspoon finely grated fresh ginger root* ‖ *3½ ounces baby spinach leaves, chopped* ‖ *large handful of fresh cilantro leaves, chopped* ‖ *2 teaspoons light olive oil* ‖ *5 garlic cloves, finely sliced* ‖ *2 teaspoons cumin seeds* ‖ *2 teaspoons mustard seeds* ‖ *1 tablespoon ground cumin* ‖ *1 teaspoon ground coriander* ‖ *1 red chile, finely chopped* ‖ *sea salt*

ONE Place the lentils in a large saucepan with the water, turmeric, and ginger. Bring to a boil. Skim off any foam that forms on the surface. **TWO** Lower the heat and cook gently for 20 minutes, stirring occasionally. Add the spinach and chopped cilantro, stir, and cook for 8–10 minutes. **THREE** Heat the oil in a small, nonstick frying pan and when it is hot add the garlic, cumin and mustard seeds, ground cumin, ground coriander, and red chile. Stir-fry over high heat for 2–3 minutes, then pour this mixture into the lentils. Stir to mix well, season, and serve immediately with rice or naan bread.

Serves 4

NUTRIENT ANALYSIS PER SERVING 248 cal – 1050 kJ – 17 g protein – 38 g carbohydrates – 2 g sugars – 4 g fat – 0 g saturated fat – 8 g fiber – 65 mg sodium

HEALTHY TIP Both lentils and spinach are an excellent source of iron, making this dish a real iron-booster. Lentils are also a great source of fiber and protein, so dhal is a great choice for a vegetarian meal.

Herbed bean and baby new potato salad

This refreshing, wholesome salad is the perfect side to grilled, spicy fish or meat dishes. The yogurt dressing is cooling too, so if you're not used to hot food, it's the perfect choice.

INGREDIENTS *8–10 small baby new potatoes* ‖ *1 garlic clove, crushed* ‖ *½ teaspoon ground cumin* ‖ *½ teaspoon ground coriander* ‖ *½ teaspoon crushed red pepper* ‖ *1 teaspoon raw sugar* ‖ *1 cup low-fat plain fromage frais or low-fat plain yogurt* ‖ *juice of 1 lime* ‖ *2 green onions, finely chopped* ‖ *½ red bell pepper, very finely diced* ‖ *3½ ounces each canned red kidney beans and black-eyed peas, rinsed and drained* ‖ *a small handful each of roughly chopped cilantro and mint leaves* ‖ *salt*

ONE Boil the potatoes until tender and halve them. Place them in a large mixing bowl and set aside. **TWO** Whisk together the garlic, cumin, coriander, crushed red pepper, sugar, yogurt, fromage frais, and lime juice. Add to the potatoes with the green onion, red bell pepper, and beans. Season well and add the chopped herbs. Toss to coat well before serving.

Serves 4

NUTRIENT ANALYSIS PER SERVING 124 cal – 526 kJ – 8 g protein – 22 g carbohydrates – 8 g sugars – 1 g fat – 0 g saturated fat – 3 g fiber – 139 mg sodium

HEALTHY TIP The good intentions of a healthy salad can often be ruined by the addition of a rich, creamy dressing—but this low-fat, yogurt-based dressing is just the thing for health-conscious eating.

Cilantro- and cumin-flecked roti

These classic flatbreads make a great alternative to chapatis for scooping up moist curries and fragrant rice. The finely chopped cilantro leaves and whole cumin seeds give the breads a lovely appearance and fabulous flavor.

INGREDIENTS *3⅔ cups whole grain flour, plus extra for dusting* ‖ *1 teaspoon salt* ‖ *3–4 teaspoons cumin seeds* ‖ *2 tablespoons very finely chopped cilantro leaves* ‖ *2–3 tablespoons light olive oil* ‖ *1 cup lukewarm water*

ONE Mix together the flour, salt, cumin, and cilantro in a large mixing bowl. Add the oil and work it into the mixture with your fingers. Gradually add the measured water and knead for 5–6 minutes until smooth, adding a little extra flour if necessary. Cover the dough with a damp cloth and let rest for 30 minutes. **TWO** Divide the dough into 16 pieces and form each into a round ball. Roll out each ball into a 5–6-inch disc, lightly dusting with flour if needed. **THREE** Heat a large cast-iron griddle pan or a heavy-bottomed frying pan over high heat. Cook the rotis, one at a time, for 45 seconds on one side, then flip over and continue to cook for 1–2 minutes until lightly browned at the edges. Remove and keep warm in aluminum foil as you continue to cook the rest. Serve warm with a variety of dishes, from fish, meat, and chicken to vegetables and salads.

Makes 16

NUTRIENT ANALYSIS PER ROTI 98 cal – 416 kJ – 3 g protein – 16 g carbohydrate – 1 g sugars – 3 g fat – 0 g saturated fat – 2 g fiber – 123 mg sodium

HEALTHY TIP Cumin is becoming recognized as a super-spice with powerful antioxidant properties. It contains a compound known as circumin, which is believed to be responsible for cumin's healing properties.

Red onion, chile, and gram flour bread

Gram flour, or *besan*, is made from ground chickpeas and can be found in large supermarkets and Asian stores. It gives these tasty, spiced flatbreads a lovely nutty flavor.

INGREDIENTS *1 cup whole grain flour* ‖ *1 cup gram flour* ‖ *1 red onion, finely diced* ‖ *1 red chile, seeded and finely chopped* ‖ *1 tablespoon chopped fresh cilantro leaves* ‖ *1 teaspoon cumin seeds* ‖ *1 teaspoon black onion seeds (nigella)* ‖ *1–1¼ cups lukewarm water* ‖ *salt* ‖ *sunflower or light olive oil, for brushing*

ONE Sift both of the flours into a large mixing bowl and add the onion, red chile, chopped cilantro, and cumin and onion seeds. Season and mix together. Gradually pour in the water and knead for 2–3 minutes on a lightly floured surface, to make a soft dough. Let rest for 5 minutes and then divide the dough into 8 pieces. Shape each one into a ball. **TWO** Roll the balls out on a lightly floured surface to a 5-inch diameter disc. **THREE** Heat a large, flat griddle pan or nonstick frying pan until it is hot. Cook the rolled-out discs of dough, one at a time, for 30 seconds on one side; brush with a little oil, flip over, and cook for 1 minute, moving the bread around. Then flip the dough over again to cook on the other side for 1 minute or until the bread is lightly browned on both sides. Remove and keep warm, wrapped in aluminum foil while you cook the remainder. Serve warm.

Makes 8

NUTRIENT ANALYSIS PER BREAD 97 cal – 412 kJ – 5 g protein – 16 g carbohydrate – 1 g sugars – 2 g fat – 0 g saturated fat – 3 g fiber – 7 mg sodium

HEALTHY TIP To ensure that you use the minimum amount of oil, use a pastry brush or paper towel moistened with oil to prevent the breads from sticking to the pan.

Southern Indian dosas with shrimp and crayfish

These crispy, light pancakes, wrapped around a hearty spiced filling, are an essential part of southern Indian dining. They're filling, though, so they can be enjoyed as a meal in themselves, served simply with Cilantro, Mint, and Coconut Chutney (*see page 129*) and perhaps a fresh, crunchy salad.

INGREDIENTS *3⅔ cups rice flour* ‖ *¼ teaspoon baking powder* ‖ *1 egg* ‖ *1 tablespoon sunflower oil* ‖ *½ teaspoon finely crushed fenugreek seeds* ‖ *salt* ‖ *sunflower oil, for brushing*

STUFFING *1 tablespoon sunflower oil* ‖ *1 teaspoon cumin seeds* ‖ *1 onion, halved and thinly sliced* ‖ *2 teaspoons finely grated fresh ginger root* ‖ *2 teaspoons finely grated garlic* ‖ *1 red chile, finely sliced* ‖ *1½ pounds cooked peeled shrimp and crayfish tails* ‖ *3 tablespoons each chopped fresh cilantro and mint leaves* ‖ *salt*

ONE Make the batter for the dosas by putting the rice flour, baking powder, egg, sunflower oil, and fenugreek in a mixing bowl. Pour in cold water, slowly, whisking all the time to give you a batter that is the consistency of heavy cream. Season, cover, and chill for 3–4 hours. **TWO** Meanwhile, make the filling. Heat the oil in a large frying pan, and when it is hot add the cumin and onion. Cook over gentle heat for 10–12 minutes or until the onion has softened, then add the ginger, garlic, and red chilli. Stir-fry for 1–2 minutes before adding the shrimp and crayfish. Stir and cook for 2–3 minutes, stir in the cilantro and mint, season, and remove from heat. Set aside and keep warm. **THREE** To make the dosas, brush a medium, nonstick frying pan with oil and set it over medium-high heat. Add a ladleful of the batter and swirl to cover the base of the pan evenly. Cook for 1–2 minutes, then flip and cook on the other side for 30 seconds. Repeat until all the batter has been used. Spoon the shrimp mixture evenly over the dosas and serve warm with Cilantro, Mint, and Coconut Chutney (*see page 129*).

Serves 4

NUTRIENT ANALYSIS PER SERVING 179 cal – 750 kJ – 10 g protein – 28 g carbohydrates – 1 g sugars – 2 g fat – 0 g saturated fat – 0 g fiber – 533 g sodium

HEALTHY TIP Fresh ginger, an essential spice in many Indian dishes, is great for stimulating circulation.

Spiced zucchini pancakes

These tasty little pancakes can be made in advance and warmed through in a low oven just before serving—so they're perfect for entertaining. Fresh, tangy raita makes a lovely contrast to the rich, melting taste of the pancakes.

INGREDIENTS *1 cup zucchini, coarsely grated* ‖ *5 ounces dried coconut* ‖ *1⅓ cups gram flour* ‖ *1 teaspoon cumin seeds* ‖ *1 red chile, finely chopped* ‖ *2 tablespoons finely chopped fresh cilantro leaves* ‖ *salt* ‖ *sunflower oil to grease the frying pan*

MINT RAITA *½ cup finely chopped mint leaves* ‖ *6 tablespoons low-fat plain yogurt* ‖ *1 teaspoon raw sugar* ‖ *salt and freshly ground black pepper*

ONE Squeeze out and discard all the liquid from the zucchini and place in a mixing bowl with the coconut, gram flour, cumin seeds, chile, and cilantro. **TWO** Add a little water to blend until you have a batter of dropping consistency. Season. **THREE** Lightly grease a nonstick frying pan with oil and set over a medium heat. Ladle a spoonful of the batter into the pan and flatten it with the back of a spoon into a 6-inch disc. Cook for 2–3 minutes and then flip the pancake over and cook for 2–3 minutes until lightly browned. Remove from the pan, transfer to a plate and while you use up the rest of the batter, keep the cooked pancakes covered in a low oven until you are ready to serve. **FOUR** To make the raita, place all the ingredients in a food processor and blend until fairly smooth. Serve the zucchini pancakes hot or cold with the mint raita.

Serves 4

NUTRIENT ANALYSIS PER SERVING 405 cal – 1688 kJ – 15 g protein – 29 g carbohydrates – 9 g sugars – 26 g fat – 20 g saturated fat – 15 g fiber – 79 mg sodium

HEALTHY TIP These golden vegetable pancakes make a terrific alternative to the crunchy deep-fried pappadams that are often served before an Indian meal in the West. They're quite filling, though, so don't eat too many.

chutneys

Cucumber and mint raita

Cool, fresh, and extremely versatile, this raita can be served as an accompaniment to almost any dish, snack, or meal. The cool cucumber and yogurt mixture acts as a perfect foil, especially for spicy food.

INGREDIENTS *1 large cucumber, peeled ‖ 1 cup low-fat yogurt ‖ 1 teaspoon caster sugar ‖ 1 red chile, seeded and finely sliced ‖ large handful of chopped mint leaves ‖ juice of ½ lime ‖ roasted cumin seeds and chili powder, to sprinkle*

ONE Halve the cucumber lengthwise. Using a teaspoon, scoop out the seeds and discard. Either very finely slice or dice the cucumber and place it in a bowl. **TWO** Whisk the yogurt and sugar until smooth and add the chile, mint leaves, and lime juice. Season, pour over the cucumber and toss to coat. Chill until ready to serve. Sprinkle with the cumin seeds and chili powder just before serving.

Makes about 1¾ cups

NUTRIENT ANALYSIS PER TABLESPOON SERVING 53 cal – 220 kJ – 4 g protein – 7 g carbohydrates – 7 g sugars – 1 g fat – 0 g saturated fat – 0 g fiber – 55 mg sodium

HEALTHY TIP Cucumber has a high water content and is very low in calories, making it the perfect food for anyone on a diet. Raw cucumbers can be hard to digest, but here the seeds are removed, making them easier to stomach.

Date, apricot, and raisin chutney

A no-cook, flavor-packed, sweet and spicy chutney that will liven up any dish you serve it with. Golden raisins can be substituted for the raisins in this recipe if desired. The chutney can be stored in the fridge for up to 1 week.

INGREDIENTS *¾ cup dried dates* ‖ *½ cup dried apricots* ‖ *1 tablespoon tamarind paste* ‖ *3 tablespoons organic tomato ketchup* ‖ *1 teaspoon ground coriander* ‖ *2 teaspoons raw sugar* ‖ *1 teaspoon hot chili powder* ‖ *1 tablespoon chopped fresh mint leaves* ‖ *1 cup water* ‖ *¼ cup raisins* ‖ *salt*

ONE Finely chop the dates and apricots and place them in a food processor with the tamarind paste, ketchup, ground coriander, sugar, chili powder, and mint leaves. **TWO** Add the water and blend the mixture in the processor until combined but still slightly chunky. Scrape the mixture down the sides of the processor and blend again for 1–2 minutes. **THREE** Transfer the date mixture to a bowl and stir in the raisins. Season, cover, and chill until ready to serve.

Makes about 1½ cups

NUTRIENT ANALYSIS PER TABLESPOON SERVING 56 cal – 240 kJ – 1 g protein – 14 g carbohydrates – 14 g sugars – 0.25 g fat – 0 g saturated fat – 2 g fiber – 67 mg sodium

HEALTHY TIP Dried fruits such as dates, apricots, and raisins are packed with iron, magnesium, and antioxidants. They're also very high in natural fruit sugars, so should not be eaten in excess – but a spoonful or two of this delicious chutney can only do you good!

Tamarind and red pepper chutney

This delicious sweet, sour, and spicy chutney can be used as an accompaniment to many starters and snacks. I use it to give an ordinary ham and cheese sandwich a special extra "kick."

INGREDIENTS *3½-ounce block of tamarind* ‖ *1¾ cups hot water* ‖ *¼ cup grated jaggery or palm sugar* ‖ *2 ounces brown sugar* ‖ *½ red bell pepper, finely diced* ‖ *6–8 black peppercorns* ‖ *1 teaspoon red chili powder* ‖ *1 teaspoon sea salt* ‖ *2 teaspoons cumin seeds* ‖ *1 teaspoon ground cumin* ‖ *½ teaspoon garam masala*

ONE Place the block of tamarind in a saucepan with the water and bring to a boil. Reduce the heat and cook gently for 20 minutes until the tamarind has broken down and become pulpy. Remove from the heat and strain into a saucepan through a fine metal strainer, pressing down to extract as much liquid as possible. **TWO** Add the jaggery, brown sugar, red bell pepper, black peppercorns, chili powder, salt, cumin seeds, ground cumin, and garam masala to the tamarind liquid. Cook over low heat for 15–20 minutes, stirring often. Remove from heat and let cool before pouring it into a sterilized jar. This chutney will keep up to two weeks if stored in the refrigerator.

Makes 1 cup

NUTRIENT ANALYSIS PER TABLESPOON SERVING 82 cal – 349 kJ – 1 g protein – 20 g carbohydrate – 19 g sugars – 0.3 g fat – 0 g saturated fat – 0 g fiber – 206 mg sodium

HEALTHY TIP Red bell peppers are an excellent source of vitamin C and the immune-boosting antioxidant betacarotene.

Quick lemon pickle

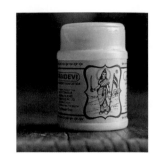

This quick pickle is made on the day you intend to use it, but it can be stored in an airtight jar or container in the refrigerator for 3–4 days. It makes a perfect accompaniment to any rice, lentil, or vegetable dish.

INGREDIENTS *1 tablespoon sunflower oil* ‖ *1 teaspoon black mustard seeds* ‖ *6–8 curry leaves* ‖ *2 dried red chiles, roughly crushed* ‖ *2 tablespoons white wine vinegar* ‖ *10 ounces preserved or pickled lemons, roughly chopped* ‖ *pinch of ground asafoetida* ‖ *sea salt*

ONE Heat the oil in a nonstick frying pan and when it is hot, add the mustard seeds. When they start to "pop," add the curry leaves and dried red chiles. Remove from heat and add the vinegar and the chopped lemon. **TWO** Return the pan to the heat and cook over medium heat for 3–4 minutes. Add the asafoetida, season well, and remove from the heat. Allow to cool completely before serving.

Makes about 1½ cups

NUTRIENT ANALYSIS PER TABLESPOON SERVING 211 kJ – 50 kcal – 1 g protein – 3 g carbohydrate – 1 g sugars – 3 g fat – 0 g saturates – 1 g fiber – 6 mg sodium

HEALTHY TIP Traditional lemon pickle is very salty, but this light, fresh version uses less salt, so is better for your health. It won't keep as well, but it's so simple to make that it's worth making it fresh.

Fresh tomato relish

Quick to prepare and packed with summer flavors, this zesty, fresh relish resembles a salsa in its consistency. Serve it with almost anything from kebabs and rice dishes to breads.

INGREDIENTS *1 pound ripe plum tomatoes, seeded and finely chopped* ‖ *½ small red onion, finely diced* ‖ *2 garlic cloves, finely diced* ‖ *1 jalapeño, seeded if desired, sliced very thinly* ‖ *small handful of chopped cilantro leaves* ‖ *juice of 2 limes* ‖ *salt*

ONE Place the tomatoes, onion and garlic in a bowl. **TWO** Add the jalapeño and cilantro leaves to the tomato mixture. **THREE** Add the lime juice, season, cover, and let sit at room temperature for 30 minutes before serving to allow the flavors to develop.

Serves 4

NUTRIENT ANALYSIS PER TABLESPOON SERVING 9 cal – 37 kJ – 0 g protein – 2 g carbohydrates – 1 g sugars – 1 g fat – 0 g saturated fat – 0.5 g fiber – 4 mg sodium

HEALTHY TIP Every ingredient in this fresh, piquant relish is packed with goodness. Tomatoes are rich in the super-phytochemical lycopene; onions, chiles, and garlic are great immunity-boosters; cilantro contains useful flavonoids; and limes provide vitamin C.

Cilantro, mint, and coconut chutney

This fresh, flavor-packed herb, coconut, and spiced chutney can be served with snacks, as a dipping sauce, or as a relish to spoon over grilled and barbecued fish and meat dishes. It will keep in the refrigerator for up to 1 week.

INGREDIENTS *1 bunch chopped fresh cilantro leaves* ‖ *½ cup chopped mint leaves* ‖ *¼ cup freshly grated coconut* ‖ *1 teaspoon finely grated fresh ginger root* ‖ *2 garlic cloves, crushed* ‖ *4–6 jalapeños (seeded), chopped* ‖ *2 tablespoons ground cashews* ‖ *1 teaspoon amchoor, or dried mango powder* ‖ *juice of ½ lemon* ‖ *1–2 teaspoons raw sugar* ‖ *½ cup low-fat plain yogurt* ‖ *salt*

ONE Place all the ingredients in a food processor and blend for 3–4 minutes until smooth. Season to taste and pour into a jar or bowl, cover, and chill until ready to use.

Makes 1 x 13-ounce jar

NUTRIENT ANALYSIS PER TABLESPOON SERVING 40 cal – 167 kJ – 2 g protein – 3 g carbohydrates – 2 g sugars – 3 g fat – 1 g saturated fat – 0.4 g fiber – 14 mg sodium

HEALTHY TIP This chutney makes a great alternative to classic Western dips, which are often based on high-fat, creamy ingredients, such as mayonnaise. Serve with little wedges of grilled flatbread, or even crunchy vegetable crudités.

Mango and nigella pickle
This pickle is really quick to prepare and makes a great addition to any rice and curry dish. Raw green mangoes are widely available from any good Asian market.

INGREDIENTS *1 pound raw green mangoes, washed, stoned, and cut into ½-inch pieces* ‖ *2 teaspoons coarse red chili powder* ‖ *2 garlic cloves, finely chopped* ‖ *6 tablespoons raw sugar* ‖ *¼ cup white wine vinegar* ‖ *2 teaspoons nigella (black onion seeds)* ‖ *2 teaspoons sea salt*

ONE Place all the ingredients in a small saucepan and cook over medium heat for about 10 minutes. Remove from heat, stir, and let cool. **TWO** When cool, pour into a sterilized jar and cover. It will keep for up to a week in the refrigerator.

Serves 4

NUTRIENT ANALYSIS PER SERVING 138 cal – 587 kJ – 1.25 g protein – 33.4 g carbohydrates – 25 .5g sugars – 1 g fat – 0.25 g saturated fat – 0.25 g fiber – 1021.5 mg sodium

HEALTHY TIP Mangoes are an excellent source of vitamin C, carotenoids, fiber, and potassium. Some studies have shown that they have the ability to improve general health and boost immunity.

Shallot thoran
This wonderful, fresh *thoran* is a lightly cooked "salad," or relish, that accompanies nearly every southern Indian meal to provide a crunchy contrast to the saucy "wet" dishes.

INGREDIENTS *2 tablespoons light olive oil* ‖ *1 teaspoon black mustard seeds* ‖ *1 teaspoon urad dhal* ‖ *8–10 curry leaves* ‖ *½ pound shallots, finely diced* ‖ *1 red chile, seeded and finely diced* ‖ *½ cup freshly grated coconut* ‖ *salt*

ONE Heat the oil in a nonstick frying pan and when hot add the mustard seeds. As soon as they start to "pop," add the urad dhal and stir-fry for 1–2 minutes, until the dhal turns a golden brown. **TWO** Add the curry leaves, shallots, and red chile and stir-fry over medium heat for 5 minutes or until the shallots have softened slightly. Add the grated coconut, stir-fry for 1–2 minutes, then remove the pan from the heat. Season and serve.

Serves 4

NUTRIENT ANALYSIS PER TABLESPOON SERVING 170 cal – 707 kJ – 2 g protein – 7 g carbohydrates – 5 g sugars – 15 g fat – 9 g saturated fat – 4 g fiber – 7 mg sodium

HEALTHY TIP Shallots belong to the same family as garlic. Some scientific studies have shown that members of the allium family increase the levels of good cholestrol in the body. This good cholestrol helps to carry the bad cholestrol away from the arteries in our bodies and so may help reduce the risk of heart disease.

drinks

Mango, cardomom, and chile ice

Beautifully flavored, with a hidden "kick" from the chili powder, this ice made from the sweetest mangoes and gently spiced with crushed cardomom seeds, will have you wishing for more.

INGREDIENTS *5 large, ripe sweet mangoes, peeled, stoned and flesh removed, or 1 cup fresh mango purée* ‖ *1 teaspoon crushed cardomom seeds* ‖ *¼ teaspoon chili powder* ‖ *1 cup low-fat vanilla yogurt* ‖ *wedges of fresh cherries or fresh mango, to serve (optional)*

ONE Place the flesh of the mango in a food processor with the cardomom seeds, chili powder and yogurt. **TWO** Blend until smooth, then pour the contents into an ice-cream maker and follow the manufacturer's instructions. **THREE** If you don't have an ice-cream maker, place the contents in a freezer-proof container, cover, and freeze for 2–3 hours. Using a fork, break up the crystals that form toward the side of the container and stir to break up the mixture. Repeat this step 4–5 times (every 30 minutes or so) until the mixture is smooth and firm. Cover and freeze until ready to serve. **FOUR** Remove the ice cream from the freezer 10–15 minutes before serving and then scoop it into short dessert glasses or bowls and serve with wedges of fresh cherries or fresh mango if desired.

Serves 4

NUTRIENT ANALYSIS PER SERVING 154 cal – 660 kJ – 3 g protein – 36 g carbohydrates – 35 g sugars – 1 g fat – 0 g saturated fat – 0 g fiber – 39 mg sodium

HEALTHY TIP Chiles are rich in carotenoids and vitamin C and are thought to help increase blood flow. They also have antibacterial properties, which make them a favorite for beating colds and the flu.

Carrot halwa

This dessert has a fudge-like texture and delicious flavor and is usually made on special feast and festival days in India.

INGREDIENTS *4 cups 2 percent milk* ‖ *2 cups coarsely grated carrots* ‖ *¼ cup unsalted butter* ‖ *1 tablespoon golden syrup or corn syrup* ‖ *½ cup golden caster sugar* ‖ *½ cup golden raisins* ‖ *4 cardamom pods, lightly crushed* ‖ *½ teaspoon ground cinnamon* ‖ *low-fat yogurt or crème fraîche, to serve (optional)*

ONE Place the milk, carrots, butter, golden syrup, caster sugar, raisins, cardamom pods, and cinnamon in a heavy-bottomed saucepan. Bring to a boil. Reduce the heat and cook gently for 20–25 minutes, stirring often. **TWO** Remove from heat and serve warm or allow the mixture to cool and serve it chilled with a dollop of low-fat yogurt or crème fraîche on the side.

Serves 4

NUTRIENT ANALYSIS PER SERVING 465 cal – 1964 kJ – 10 g protein – 79 g carbohydrates – 78 g sugars – 15 g fat – 9 g saturated fat – 5 g fiber – 200 mg sodium

HEALTHY TIP Carrots are known to have great blood-purifying qualities and are packed with vitamin D. They are even more nutritious cooked than raw. This is because the cell walls of raw carrots are tough and the cooking process helps break them down to make the betacarotene (the vegetable equivalent of vitamin A) easier for the body to absorb.

Minted melon fruit salad with ginger

Light and refreshing, this flavorsome fruit salad is the perfect way to end a meal and will help to cleanse the palate. The addition of ginger gives it a real bite and helps to enhance the delicate flavor of the melon. If charantais melon is not available, increase the amount of the other three melons.

INGREDIENTS *1 honeydew melon, about ¾ pound* ‖ *1 charantais melon, about ¾ pound* ‖ *½ small watermelon, about ¾ pound* ‖ *1 cantaloupe melon, about ¾ pound* ‖ *2 tablespoons finely chopped stem ginger* ‖ *2 tablespoons syrup from the stem ginger* ‖ *1 tablespoon lemon juice* ‖ *3 tablespoons very finely chopped mint leaves*

ONE Peel, seed, and cut the flesh of the melons into bite-sized cubes or, using a melonballer, scoop out balls, reserving any juices from the fruit. Place the fruit and any juices in a large serving bowl. **TWO** Sprinkle the stem ginger, syrup, lemon juice, and mint leaves over the fruit. Toss to mix well and, if time permits, chill for 30 minutes before serving.

Serves 4

NUTRIENT ANALYSIS PER SERVING

259 cal – 1109 kJ – 5 g protein – 60 g carbohydrates – 60 g sugars – 2 g fat – 0 g saturated fat – 7 g fiber – 207 mg sodium

HEALTHY TIP Melons are a natural diuretic and have a cleansing effect on the digestive system. Orange- and red-fleshed melons, such as cantaloupe and watermelon, also contain health-promoting betacarotene.

Watermelon, lime, chile, and vodka granitas

Icy cool, with a kick from the chile and vodka, this unusual dessert has a slushy consistency and is perfect after a fiery meal.

INGREDIENTS *½ small watermelon, cut into cubes and seeds discarded* ‖ *¼ cup raw sugar* ‖ *1 teaspoon finely diced red chile* ‖ *½ cup water* ‖ *juice and finely grated zest of 1 lime* ‖ *3 tablespoons vodka*

ONE Put the melon in a food processor and blend until smooth. **TWO** Place the sugar, chile, and the water in a small saucepan and bring to a boil. Reduce the heat, add the lime juice and zest, and gently simmer for 1 minute, stirring until all the sugar has dissolved. Remove from heat and when cool add to the watermelon mixture with the vodka. Blend until smooth and then transfer the mixture to a wide freezer-proof container. Cover and freeze for 4–5 hours. **THREE** To serve, remove from the freezer and stir the mixture vigorously with a fork to break it up into a mass of small ice crystals. Alternatively, you can place the frozen mixture in the food processor and pulse briefly until you have a slushy consistency. Spoon the mixture into frozen glasses and serve immediately.

Serves 4

NUTRIENT ANALYSIS PER SERVING 133 cal – 563 kJ – 1 g protein – 27 g carbohydrates – 27 g sugars – 1 g fat – 0 g saturated fat – 1 g fiber – 3 mg sodium

HEALTHY TIP Granitas, which are rather like a slushy sorbet, make a much healthier choice than ice cream. They're virtually fat-free, and this version contains very little sugar, relying on the natural sweetness of the watermelon instead.

Sweet vermicelli with saffron and nuts

Known as *seviyan*, this is a classic Indian dessert, which is just as good as an indulgent sweet snack as it is when enjoyed after a meal. The saffron gives it a warm, spiced flavor and a rich golden color.

INGREDIENTS *2 tablespoons light olive oil* ‖ *4 ounces brown rice vermicelli* ‖ *3 cups 2 percent milk* ‖ *large pinch of saffron threads* ‖ *½ teaspoon crushed cardamom seeds* ‖ *6 tablespoons raw sugar* ‖ *¾ cup raisins* ‖ *½ cup chopped mixed nuts, to serve*

ONE Heat the oil in a heavy-bottomed saucepan. Break the vermicelli into 1½-inch lengths and place it in the pan. Stir-fry over gentle heat for 4–5 minutes until lightly golden, then pour in the milk and bring it to a boil. **TWO** Add the saffron, cardamom, and sugar; stir and cook over medium heat for 15–20 minutes until thickened. Add the raisins, stir, and cook for 2–3 minutes, then remove from heat. **THREE** Transfer the mixture into individual bowls, let cool, and chill for 3–4 hours. Sprinkle with the nuts and serve immediately.

Serves 4

NUTRIENT ANALYSIS PER SERVING 600 cal – 2523 kJ – 17 g protein – 91 g carbohydrates – 65 g sugars – 21 g fat – 5 g saturated fat – 5 g fiber – 140 mg sodium

HEALTHY TIP Traditionally *seviyan* is made with butter and whole milk, but this modern version uses healthy monounsaturated olive oil and 2 percent milk. Brown rice vermicelli is high in fiber and contains no cholesterol.

Pistachio and raisin ground rice pudding

Using ground rice for this pudding gives it a smooth, creamy texture that contrasts well with the plump, juicy raisins and the bite of the pale green pistachios.

INGREDIENTS *½ cup coarsely ground rice flour ‖ ¼ teaspoon cardamom seeds, crushed ‖ 3¾ cups semi-skimmed milk ‖ 6 tablespoons raw sugar ‖ 1 tablespoon rose water ‖ ¼ cup chopped pistachios ‖ 2 tablespoons golden raisins*

TO DECORATE *pistachios, golden raisins*

ONE Place the rice in a saucepan with the cardamom and 2 cups of the milk. Bring to a boil, stirring often. **TWO** Add the remaining milk and cook over medium heat for 10–12 minutes or until the mixture thickens slightly. Stir in the sugar and rosewater and continue to cook for 2–3 minutes. **THREE** Stir in the pistachios and golden raisins and transfer the mixture into 4 individual bowls. Chill for 3–4 hours, then serve, decorated with chopped pistachios and golden raisins.

Serves 4

NUTRIENT ANALYSIS PER SERVING 357 cal – 1507 kJ – 12 g protein – 53 g carbohydrates – 41 g sugars – 12 g fat – 2 g saturated fat – 1 g fiber – 127 mg sodium

HEALTHY TIP Rice pudding made with 2 percent milk is a healthy dessert choice. The golden raisins are naturally sweet, so you don't need to add as much sugar as you would for a regular rice pudding.

Papaya and pomegranate fruit salad

Sprinkling black pepper over sweet, juicy fruit really helps to bring out its taste. This stunning, jewel-like fruit salad is packed with flavor and color and is very refreshing.

INGREDIENTS *1 large ripe papaya or 2 smaller ones, seeded and cut into bite-sized cubes* ‖ *1 pomegranate* ‖ *2 teaspoons honey* ‖ *juice of 1 lime* ‖ *¼ teaspoon crushed black pepper* ‖ *1 tablespoon ginger wine* ‖ *mint leaves, to decorate (optional)*

ONE Place the prepared papaya in a large, shallow serving bowl. **TWO** Cut the pomegranate in half widthwise and remove the seeds (the easiest way to do this is to tap the fruit with a heavy spoon and allow the seeds to drop off). Add to the papaya and mix well. **THREE** Put the honey, lime juice, pepper, and ginger wine into a small bowl and stir to mix well. Drizzle this over the fruit and gently toss to mix well. Decorate with mint leaves before serving, if liked.

Serves 4

NUTRIENT ANALYSIS PER SERVING 100 cal – 423 kJ – 1 g protein – 25 g carbohydrates – 4 g sugars – 0 g fat – 0 g saturated fat – 0 g fiber – 8 mg sodium

HEALTHY TIP Papayas are an excellent choice for dessert. They contain the enzyme papain, which is said to help the digestion of protein.

Almond milk sherbet

Also known as *thandai*, this cool, milky, soothing drink is usually drunk at religious festivals and on special occasions such as Holi (the festival of spring) and Divali (the festival of lights).

INGREDIENTS *1 cup ground almonds* ‖ *½ teaspoon crushed cardamom seeds* ‖ *pinch of grated nutmeg* ‖ *¼ cup raw sugar* ‖ *pinch of turmeric (optional)* ‖ *6 cups 2 percent milk*

ONE Place all the ingredients in a heavy-bottomed saucepan and bring to a boil. Remove from the heat and let infuse for 15–20 minutes. **TWO** Strain the mixture through a fine metal strainer and chill for 5–6 hours, or overnight. **THREE** To serve, fill 4 tall glasses with ice and pour in the almond sherbet.

Serves 4

NUTRIENT ANALYSIS PER SERVING 519 cal – 2215 kJ – 23 g protein – 36 g carbohydrates – 34 g sugars – 34 g fat – 6 g saturated fat – 6 g fiber – 213 g sodium

HEALTHY TIP Although the addition of ground almonds boosts the fat and calorie content of this drink, almonds also add B vitamins and other useful nutrients, making this a much healthier choice than a high-fat milkshake made with ice cream.

Masala chai

This mildly spiced and soothing tea is a traditional Indian favorite. It is drunk and served all over India, from little street stalls, to bustling stations and other public places. On trains, it is served in little clay cups. which adds to the flavor in a strange kind of way.

INGREDIENTS *1-inch piece of fresh ginger root, roughly chopped* ‖ *6 cloves* ‖ *1-inch piece of cassia bark or cinnamon stick* ‖ *4 cardamom pods* ‖ *2 cups water* ‖ *1 cup 2 percent milk* ‖ *3 tablespoons loose Indian tea (Darjeeling or Assam)* ‖ *2 tablespoons raw sugar*

ONE Place all the ingredients in a heavy-bottomed saucepan. **TWO** Bring the mixture to a boil, reduce the heat, and allow it to cook gently for 2–3 minutes. **THREE** Remove from heat and strain the mixture, using a fine strainer. Pour the chai into cups or heatproof glasses and serve hot.

Serves 4

NUTRIENT ANALYSIS PER SERVING 226 cal – 959 kJ – 8 g protein – 44 g carbohydrates – 42 g sugars – 3 g fat – 2 g saturated fat – 0 g fiber – 113 mg sodium

HEALTHY TIP The aromatic spices in this drink not only add flavor but also have healing properties. Ginger stimulates the circulation, while cardamom is said to help relieve nausea and indigestion and is also used to treat colds.

Strawberry lassi

Cool, creamy lassi is the classic drink enjoyed throughout India, where it is served either salty or sweet. This sweet version is made with strawberries and flavored with rose water and is absolutely delicious.

INGREDIENTS *1 pint strawberries, roughly chopped* ‖ *1 cup low-fat plain yogurt* ‖ *2 tablespoons raw sugar* ‖ *3 cups ice cold water* ‖ *a few drops of rose water* ‖ *coarsely ground black pepper, to serve*

ONE Place the strawberries in a food processor with half the ice water. Blend until smooth. **TWO** Add the yogurt, sugar, remaining water, and the rose water and blend until smooth and frothy. Pour into chilled, tall glasses, sprinkle with black pepper, and serve immediately.

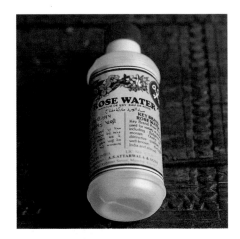

Serves 4

NUTRIENT ANALYSIS PER SERVING 99 cal – 416 kJ – 5 g protein – 20 g carbohydrates – 20 g sugars – 1 g fat – 0 g saturated fat – 2 g fiber – 68 mg sodium

HEALTHY TIP If you're in a hurry and haven't got time for a proper breakfast, this healthy, sustaining drink makes an excellent alternative.

Carrot, ginger, and beet juice

It is essential to have a good fruit and vegetable juicer for this recipe, as it will extract all the nutrients from the ingredients in a smooth and silky manner. You can vary this juice by using 4–6 apples instead of the beets.

INGREDIENTS *10 large organic carrots* ‖ *4 large beets* ‖ *1-inch piece of fresh ginger root*

ONE Put the vegetables through a juicer and extract all the juice. **TWO** Strain if desired and serve immediately.

Serves 4

NUTRIENT ANALYSIS PER SERVING 133 cal – 560 kJ – 4 g protein – 29 g carbohydrates – 27 g sugars – 1 g fat – 0 g saturated fat – 1 g fiber – 155 mg sodium

HEALTHY TIP Beets are full of folic acid and manganese, and carrot juice is full of biotin, which helps to maintain hair, nerves, and skin.

Iced cardamom coffee

This aromatic, sweetly spiced coffee is delicious at any time of day—first thing in the morning, after lunch, midafternoon, or even in the evening.

INGREDIENTS *5–6 cardamom pods, roughly crushed* ‖ *1-inch piece of cassia bark or cinnamon stick* ‖ *1¼ cups 2 percent milk* ‖ *1¼ cups good, strong black coffee, chilled* ‖ *sugar, to taste (optional)* ‖ *single cream or vanilla ice cream, to serve (optional)*

ONE Place the cardamom pods in a heavy-bottomed saucepan with the cassia or cinnamon and the milk. Bring to a boil, remove from heat, and allow to infuse until cooled. **TWO** Put the chilled coffee in a blender and strain the spiced milk into it. Blend until smooth, stir in sugar to taste, if using, and return the mixture to the refrigerator; chill for 2–3 hours. **THREE** To serve, pour the chilled coffee mixture into chilled, ice-filled glasses. Top the glasses with a small spoonful of whipped cream or a small scoop of vanilla ice cream.

Serves 4

NUTRIENT ANALYSIS PER SERVING 36 cal – 152 kJ – 3 g protein – 4 g carbohydrates – 4 g sugars – 1 g fat – 1 g saturated fat – 0 g fiber – 42 mg sodium

HEALTHY TIP If you're watching your weight or keeping an eye on your fat intake, don't add the cream or ice cream to this coffee. It's just as good without.

Mint and lemongrass tea

In India, a varied assortment of herbs and spices are added to hot water or milk to make a selection of teas that are considered detoxifying. This particular tea has a fresh, clean fragrance—perfect for cleansing the palate.

INGREDIENTS *3 cups water* ‖ *4 lemongrass stalks, lightly crushed to release the oils* ‖ *small handful of mint leaves* ‖ *1 tablespoon honey (optional)*

ONE Bring the water to a boil in a large saucepan. Add the lemongrass stalks and boil for 5–6 minutes; remove from heat. **TWO** Add the mint leaves and honey, if using, cover and allow to infuse for 10 minutes. **THREE** Serve in cups or glasses or chilled in a tall glass with plenty of ice.

Serves 4

NUTRIENT ANALYSIS PER SERVING 1 cal – 5 kJ – 0 g protein – 0 g carbohydrates – 0 g sugars – 0 g fat – 0 g saturated fat – 0 g fiber – 0 mg sodium

HEALTHY TIP This calming tea stimulates digestion, so it is perfect for serving to guests after a large meal.

Index

Acknowledgments

EXECUTIVE EDITOR Nicky Hill

PROJECT EDITOR Kate Tuckett

EXECUTIVE ART EDITOR AND DESIGN Geoff Fennell

PHOTOGRAPHY Jason Lowe/© Octopus Publishing Group Ltd

PRODUCTION MANAGER Ian Paton

FOOD STYLIST Sunil Vijayakar